Eyewitness
OIL

PLEASE CHECK FOR CD

Detergent containing
petrochemicals

Roman oil lamp

Internal combustion engine

Diesel-engined freight truck

Basket of recyclable
packaging

Molecule of
polythene plastic

Fern fossil in coal

Drill bit from
oil rig

Eyewitness
OIL

Camping stove burning butane
derived from natural gas

Written by
JOHN FARNDON

Offshore oil rig

Liquid natural gas tanker

Plastic ducks

DK

LONDON, NEW YORK,
MELBOURNE, MUNICH, AND DELHI

Consultant Mike Graul

Managing editor Camilla Hallinan
Managing art editor Martin Wilson
Publishing manager Sunita Gahir
Category publisher Andrea Pinnington
Production controller Georgina Hayworth
Picture research Louise Thomas
Picture librarian Claire Bowers
DTP designers Andy Hilliard, Siu Ho, Ben Hung
Senior art editor David Ball
Jacket designer Neal Cobourne
Jacket editor Adam Powley

For Cooling Brown Ltd:
Creative director Arthur Brown
Project editor Steve Setford
Art editor Tish Jones

First published in Great Britain in 2007
by Dorling Kindersley Limited,
80 Strand, London WC2R 0RL

2 4 6 8 10 9 7 5 3
ED495 – 04/07

Copyright © 2007 Dorling Kindersley Limited
A Penguin Company

A CIP catalogue record for this book is
available from the British Library

ISBN: 978-1-40531-861-7

Colour reproduction by Colourscan, Singapore
Printed and bound in China by Toppan Printing Co. (Shenzhen) Ltd

Discover more at
www.dk.com

Paraffin lamp

Oil floating
on water

Cutaway of a
wind turbine

Magazines printed with
oil-based inks

Contents

Seismic survey truck

King oil

OUR WORLD IS RULED BY OIL. People have used oil for thousands of years, but in the last century we have begun to consume it in vast quantities. Daily oil consumption in the USA, for example, rose from a few tens of thousand barrels in 1900 to over 21 million barrels in 2000 – more than 3.3 billion litres (730 million gallons) per day. Oil is our most important energy source, providing fuel to keep our transport going, and even some of the heat needed to generate the electricity on which our modern lifestyle relies. Oil is also a raw material from which many key substances, including most plastics, are made. But we need to reassess our oil dependence, since the world's oil supplies may be gradually running out, and the scale of our oil consumption is damaging the environment.

SUPERMARKET SECRETS
People in the world's developed countries eat a wider variety of food than ever before – thanks largely to oil. Oil fuels the planes, ships, and trucks that bring food to local shops from all around the world. It also fuels the cars in which we drive to the supermarket. And it provides the plastic packaging and the energy for the refrigeration that keep the food fresh.

LIQUID ENERGY
Unprocessed liquid oil – called crude oil – is not an impressive sight, but it is a very concentrated form of energy. In fact, there is enough energy in one barrel (159 litres/35 gallons) of crude oil to boil about 2,700 litres (600 gallons) of water.

Large tankers carry 15,000–30,000 litres (3,000–6,600 gallons) or more of oil

Tough polycarbonate case protects delicate electronics inside

OIL IN THE INFORMATION AGE
A sleek, slimline laptop computer looks a million miles away from crude oil, and yet without oil it could not exist. Oil not only provides the basic raw material for the polycarbonate plastic from which a computer's case is typically made, but it also provides the energy to make most of its internal parts. Oil may even have generated the electricity used to charge the computer's batteries.

FREEDOM TO TRAVEL
Petrol produced from crude oil powers the cars that enable us to travel around with an ease and speed undreamed of in earlier times. Many commuters drive to work over distances that once took days to cover on horseback. But with over 600 million motor vehicles on the world's roads, and the figure rising daily, the amount of oil burned to achieve this mobility is truly staggering – about a billion barrels each month.

SLICK JUMPING

Oil plays a part even in the simplest and most basic activities. Skateboarding, for example, only really took off with the development of wheels made from an oil-based plastic called polyurethane, which is both tough and smooth. But the oil connection does not end there. Another plastic called expanded polystyrene, or EPS, provides a solid foam for a boarder's helmet. EPS squashes easily to absorb the impact from a fall. A third oil-based plastic, HDPE, is used to make knee and elbow protectors.

Impact-absorbing EPS helmet

Dense HDPE knee protector

Smooth, durable polyurethane wheels

Satellite view of Asia at night

NON-STOP CITIES

Seen from space at night, the world's cities twinkle in the darkness like stars in the sky. The brightness of our cities is only achieved by consuming a huge amount of energy – and much of this is obtained from oil. All this light not only makes cities safer, but it allows essential activities to go on right through the night.

Aluminium tank

OIL ON THE FARM

Farming in the developed world has been transformed by oil. With oil-powered tractors and harvesters, a farmer can work the land with a minimum of manual labour. And using an oil-powered aircraft, a single person can spray a large field with pesticide or herbicide in minutes. Even pesticides and herbicides, which increase crop yields, may be made from chemicals derived from oil.

Wheat

OIL ON THE MOVE

To sustain our oil-reliant way of life, huge quantities of oil have to be transported around the world every day – many millions of barrels of it. Some is carried across the sea in supertankers, and some is pumped through long pipelines. But most filling stations are supplied by road tankers like this. Without such tankers to keep vehicles continually supplied with petrol, countries would grind to a standstill in just a few days.

SUNTAN OIL

A century ago the furthest most people went for a holiday was a short train ride away. Now millions of people fly huge distances, often travelling half way round the world for a holiday of just a few weeks or less. But like cars and trucks, aircraft are fuelled by oil, and the amount of oil consumed by air travel is rising all the time.

Ancient oil

In many parts of the Middle East, the region's vast underground oil reserves seep to the surface in sticky black pools and lumps. People learned long ago just how useful this black substance, called bitumen (or pitch or tar), could be. Stone Age hunters used it to attach flint arrowheads to their arrows. At least 6,500 years ago, people living in the marshes of what is now Iraq learned to add bitumen to bricks and cement to waterproof their houses against floods. Soon people realized that bitumen could be used for anything from sealing water tanks to gluing broken pots. By Babylonian times, there was a massive trade in this "black gold" throughout the Middle East, and whole cities were literally built with it.

Chinese bamboo drill

THE FIRST OIL DRILLS
Not all ancient oil was found on the surface. Over 2,000 years ago in Sichuan, the Chinese began to drill wells using bamboo tipped by iron to get at brine (salty water) underground. They needed the brine to extract salt for health and preserving food. When they drilled very deep, they found not just brine but also oil and natural gas. It is not known whether the Chinese made use of the oil, but the natural gas was burned under big pans of brine to boil off the water and obtain the salt.

LEAK-STOPPERS
About 6,000 years ago, the Ubaid people of the marshy lands in what is now Iraq realized that bitumen's waterproofing qualities made it ideal for boats. They coated their reed boats with bitumen inside and out to seal them against leaks. The idea was eventually adopted by builders of wooden boats throughout the world. Known as caulking, this method was used to waterproof boats right up until the days of modern metal and glass-fibre hulls. Sailors were often called "tars", because their clothes were stained with tar (bitumen) from caulking.

Bamboo

Medieval painting of Greek fishing boat

Planks sealed together with bitumen

BLACK MUMMIES

The Ancient Egyptians preserved their dead as mummies by soaking them in a brew of chemicals such as salt, beeswax, cedar tree resin, and bitumen. The word "mummy" may come from the Arabic word *mumya*, for the Mumya Mountain in Persia where bitumen was found. Until recently, scholars believed that bitumen was never used for mummification, and that the name came simply from the way mummies turned black when exposed to air. Now, chemical analysis has shown that bitumen was indeed used in Egyptian mummies, but only during the later "Ptolemaic" period (323–30 BCE). It was shipped to Egypt from the Dead Sea, where it could be found floating on the water.

Mummified head

BABYLON BITUMEN

Most of the great buildings in Ancient Babylon relied on bitumen. To King Nebuchadnezzar (reigned 604–562 BCE), it was the most important material in the world – a visible sign of the technological achievements of his kingdom, used for everything from baths to mortar for bricks. Nowhere was it more crucial than in the Hanging Gardens, a spectacular series of roof gardens lush with flowers and trees. Bitumen was probably used as a waterproof lining for the plant beds, and also for the pipes that carried water up to them.

CARTHAGE BURNING

Bitumen is highly flammable, but it is such a strong adhesive and so good at repelling water that it was used extensively on roofs in ancient cities such as Carthage. Sited on the coast of North Africa, in what is now Tunisia, Carthage was so powerful in its heyday that it rivalled Rome. Under the great leader, Hannibal, the Carthaginians invaded Italy. Rome recovered and attacked Carthage in 146 BCE. When the Romans set Carthage alight, the bitumen on the roofs helped to ensure that the fire spread rapidly and completely destroyed the city.

The siege of Carthage

Silver coin from Carthage

Bow slung over shoulder

Quiver for carrying arrows

Oily cloth wrapped around arrowhead

FLAMING ARROWS

At first, people were only interested in the thick, sticky form of bitumen that was good for gluing and waterproofing. This was known as *iddu*, after the city of Hit or Id (in modern Iraq) where bitumen was found. A thinner form called *naft* (giving us the modern word naphthalene) burst into flames too readily to be useful. By the 6th century BCE, the Persians had realized that *naft* could be lethal in battle. Persian archers put it on their arrows to fire flaming missiles at their enemies. Much later, in the 6th century CE, the Byzantine navy developed this idea further. They used deadly fire bombs, called "Greek fire", made from bitumen mixed with sulphur and quicklime.

Frieze showing Persian archer, 510 BCE

WARM WELCOME

In the Middle Ages, when enemies tried to scale the walls of a castle or fortified town, one famous way for defenders to beat off the attackers was to pour boiling oil down on them. The first known use of boiling oil was by Jews defending the city of Jotapata against the Romans in 67 CE. Later the idea was adopted to defend castles against attack in the Middle Ages. However, the technique was probably not used very often, since oil was extremely expensive.

Oil for light

For MILLIONS OF YEARS, the only light in the long darkness of night (apart from the stars and Moon) came from flickering fires or burning sticks. Then about 70,000 years ago, prehistoric people discovered that oils burn with a bright, steady flame. They made the first oil lamps by hollowing out a stone, filling it with moss or plant fibres soaked in oil, and then setting the moss alight. Later, they found the lamp would burn longer and brighter if they lit just a fibre "wick" dipped in a dish of oil. The oil could be animal fat, beeswax, or vegetable oil from olives or sesame seeds. Sometimes it was actually petroleum, which prehistoric people found in seeps on the ground. Oil lamps remained the main source of lighting until the invention of the gas lamp in Victorian times.

PARAFFIN LAMP

For 70 years after Aimé Argand invented his lamp (see below), most oil lamps burned whale oil. This began to change with the production of a cheaper fuel called paraffin, or kerosene, from petroleum around the mid-19th century. By the early 1860s, the majority of oil lamps burned paraffin. Although fairly similar to Argand's design, a paraffin lamp has the fuel reservoir at the bottom, beneath the wick, instead of being in a separate cylinder. The size of the flame is controlled by adjusting how much of the wick extends out of the fuel reservoir.

Glass chimney to improve the air flow and protect the flame from drafts

LADIES OF THE LAMP

By the 1890s, selling paraffin for lamps was big business, so paraffin makers tried to give their product a glamorous image. The French company Saxoleine commissioned a now-famous series of posters from the artist Jules Chéret (1836–1932). These showed various attractive Parisian women going into raptures over oil lamps filled with Saxoleine fuel, which the company claimed was clean, odourless, and safe.

Glass chimney

Glass shade to distribute the light evenly

LIGHT IN EGYPT

A lamp could be made by simply drooping a wick over the edge of a stone bowl. When the bowl had to be hand-carved from stone, lamps were probably rare. Later, people learned to mass-produce bowls from pottery. They soon developed the design by pinching and pulling the edges to make a narrow neck in which the wick could lay. This is a 2,000-year-old clay lamp from Ancient Egypt.

Wick

Pool of vegetable oil

Cup to catch
oil drips

Oil inlet
tube

Reservoir of
whale oil

Ventilation holes to
supply air to the flame

Reservoir for
paraffin

Wick height
adjuster

Lid to control
burning and
cut spillage

Spout

ARGAND LAMP

In the 1780s, the Swiss physicist Aimé Argand (1750–1803) made the greatest breakthrough in lighting since the time of the Greeks. He realized that by placing a circular wick in the middle of an oil lamp and covering it with a chimney to improve the air flow, the lamp would burn ten times brighter than a candle and very cleanly. Argand's lamp quickly superseded all other oil lamps. It revolutionized home life, making rooms bright at night for the first time in history.

WHALE HUNT

Whales had been hunted for their meat for 2,000 years, but in the 18th century people in Europe and America realized that the plentiful fat of whales, especially sperm whales, also gave a light oil that would burn brightly and cleanly. Demand for whale oil for use in lamps suddenly rocketed. The New England coast of north-eastern America became the centre of a massive whaling industry, which was made famous in Herman Melville's 1851 book *Moby Dick*.

ROMAN NIGHTS

The Greeks improved lamps by putting a lid on the bowl, with just a small hole for the oil and a spout for the wick. The lid made it harder to spill the oil, and restricted the flow of air, making the oil last much longer. By the time of the Romans, every household had its array of clay and bronze lamps, often elaborately decorated. The lid of this Roman lamp shows a scene of the burning of the city of Carthage and its queen Dido.

FLAMING TORCHES

In Hollywood films, medieval castles are illuminated at night by flaming torches mounted in wall brackets called sconces. The torches were bundles of sticks dipped in resin or pitch to make them burn brighter. In fact, torches were probably used only for special banquets, like this illustration of the Torch Dance in the *Golf Book* by Simon Bening of Bruges, c.1500 (the torch bearers are on the far left). For everyday light, people used lamps like those of the Ancient Egyptians, or simple rush lights – burning tapers made from rushes dipped in animal fat.

Dawn of the oil age

For a thousand years, people in the Middle East had been distilling oil to make paraffin for lamps, using small flasks called alembics. However, the modern oil age began in 1853, when a Polish chemist named Ignacy Lukasiewicz (1822–82) discovered how to do this on an industrial scale. In 1856, he set up the world's first crude oil refinery at Ulaszowice in Poland. Canadian Abraham Gesner (1791–1864) had managed to make paraffin from coal in 1846, but oil yielded it in larger quantities and more cheaply. Paraffin quickly replaced the more expensive whale oil as the main lamp fuel in North America and Europe. The rising demand for paraffin produced a scramble to find new sources of oil – especially in the USA.

Seneca Oil Company
stock certificate

Edwin L. Drake

"THE YANKEE HAS STRUCK OIL!"
New York lawyer George Bissell (1812–84) was sure that liquid oil below ground could be tapped by drilling. He formed Seneca Oil and hired Edwin L. Drake (1818–80), a retired railroad conductor, to go to Titusville, Pennsylvania, where water wells were often contaminated by oil. On 28 August 1859, Drake's men drilled down 21 m (70 ft) – and struck oil to create the USA's first oil well.

THE BLACK CITY
Drilled in 1847, the world's first oil well was at Baku on the Caspian Sea, in what is now Azerbaijan. Baku soon boomed with the new demand for oil. Wells were sunk by the hundred to tap into the vast underground reserves of liquid oil nearby. Known as the Black City, Baku was producing 90 per cent of the world's oil by the 1860s. This painting by Herbert Ruland shows Baku in 1960. Baku is still a major oil centre.

Powered by an electric motor, a pair of cranks raise and lower one end of the driving beam

Oil Springs,
Ontario, 1862

OIL BY THE BUCKET
In 1858, James Williams (1818–90) realized that the oily black swamps of Lambton County in Ontario, Canada, might be a source of petroleum for paraffin. He dug a hole and found that oil bubbled up so readily that he could fill bucket after bucket. This was the first oil well in the Americas. The area became known as Oil Springs, and within a few years it was dotted with simple "derricks" – frames for supporting the drilling equipment.

Signal Hill oil field, California, USA, 1935

THE OIL FOREST
Initially, the hunt for oil was a free-for-all, with many thousands of individuals risking all to try and strike it rich. As each prospector claimed a share of the spoils, the oil fields (areas of subterranean oil reserves) soon became covered by forests of oil wells and their tower-like derricks.

SPINDLETOP DRILLERS
Most early oil wells were shallow, and the oil could only be pumped up in small quantities. Then in 1901, oil workers at Spindletop in Texas, USA, were drilling more than 300 m (1,000 ft) down when they were overwhelmed by a fountain of mud and oil that erupted from the drill hole. This was Texas's first "gusher", where oil is forced up from underground by its own natural pressure. When naturally pressurized like this, oil can gush forth in enormous quantities.

The curved end of the beam is likened to a donkey's head

NODDING DONKEY
In the early days, the main sources of oil were only just below the surface. Countless wells were dug to get at it. Sometimes, the oil came up under its own natural pressure at first. But once enough oil was removed, the pressure dropped and the oil had to be pumped up. The typical pump was nicknamed a "nodding donkey" because of the way its driving-beam swung slowly up and down. As the "head" end of the beam falls, the pump's plunger goes down into the well. When the head rises, the plunger draws oil to the surface.

FIRE DRILL
The pioneering oil business was fraught with danger, and claimed the lives of many oil workers. Perhaps the greatest threat was fire. Refineries blew up, oil tanks burned down, and well heads constantly burst into flames. Once a gusher caught fire, it was very hard to put out, because the fire was constantly fed with oil from below. This burning gusher at Jennings, Louisiana, USA, was photographed in 1902.

Driving beam operates the plunger in the well shaft as it rises and falls

Nodding donkeys are still a common sight in oil fields

Petroleum Center, Pennsylvania, USA, 1873

BOOM TOWNS
As more and more oil wells were sunk, so whole new towns grew up to house the ever-growing armies of oil workers. Oil towns were rough, ramshackle places thrown up almost overnight. They reeked of petrol fumes and were black with oil waste. Some were quite literally "boom towns", since the reckless storage of nitroglycerine used to blast open wells meant that explosions were frequent.

The oil bonanza

Bordino steam car, 1854

STEAMED OUT

Some early cars had steam engines, not internal combustion engines like most cars today. This one, built by Virginio Bordino (1804–79) in 1854, burned coal to boil water into steam. Later steam cars burned petrol or paraffin, and were far more effective, but it still took about 30 minutes to get up steam before they could move. With internal combustion engine cars, a driver could just "get in and go" – especially after the invention of the electric starter motor in 1903.

NOTHING TRANSFORMED THE OIL INDUSTRY more than the arrival of the motor car in America. In 1900, there were just 8,000 cars on US roads. Car ownership reached 125,000 in 1908, and soared to 8.1 million by 1920. In 1930, there were 26.7 million cars in the USA – all of which needed fuel, and that fuel was petrol made from oil. There was huge money to be made in oil. Soon speculative prospectors known as "wildcatters" were drilling anywhere in America where there was a hint that oil might be lurking. Many went broke, but the lucky ones made their fortunes by striking "gushers". Oil from California, Oklahoma, and especially Texas fuelled a tremendous economic growth that soon made America the world's richest country. As car manufacturers and oil companies prospered, the oil bonanza transformed America forever.

T-TIME

American Henry Ford (1863–1947) dreamt of making "a motor car for the great multitude – a car so low in price that no man making a good salary will be unable to own one." The result was Ford's Model T, the world's first mass-produced car. Launched in 1908, the T was an instant success. Within five years, there were a quarter of a million Model Ts, amounting to 50 per cent of all the cars in the USA. In 1925, still half of all American cars were Model Ts, but by now there were 15 million of them. The Model T created the first big boom in oil consumption.

MASS-PRODUCTION

Cars were the toys of the rich in the early 1900s. Each car was hand-built by craftsmen, and hugely expensive. All that changed with the invention of mass-production. In mass-production, cars were not built individually. Instead, vast teams of workers added components as partly assembled cars were pulled past on factory production lines. Made like this, cars could be produced cheaply and in large quantities. Mass-production turned the car into an everyday mode of transport for ordinary Americans.

The wings could be simply bolted on in seconds as the car passed along the production line

The wheels were fitted early in the production process, so that the chassis could be moved easily along the line

The key to the T's construction was its sturdy chassis of vanadium steel

Every pump had an illuminated top to make it easy to see at night

FILL HER UP!

As more and more Americans took to the wheel in the 1920s, so roadside filling stations sprang up the length and breadth of the country to satisfy the cars' insatiable thirst for fuel. In those days, cars had smaller tanks, and could not travel so far between fill-ups. Consequently, virtually every village, neighbourhood, and small town, had a filling station, each with its own distinctive pumps designed in the oil company's style. These 1920s filling stations are now a cherished piece of America's motoring heritage.

The Gilmore company was founded by a Los Angeles dairy farmer after he struck oil while drilling for water for his cows

Old pumps are now collectors' items, often changing hands for thousands of pounds

Display shows the amount sold in US dollars

Lower counter records fuel flow

Hose delivers fuel from underground storage tank

ROARING OIL
As oil companies vied for the new business, each company tried to create its own unique brand image. Often, the image was nothing to do with oil. Instead it was an idea that made the oil seem more attractive or exciting. This 1930s pump from the Gilmore company, associating its petrol with a lion's roar, was typical. Nowadays such brand imaging is common, but in the 1920s it was new.

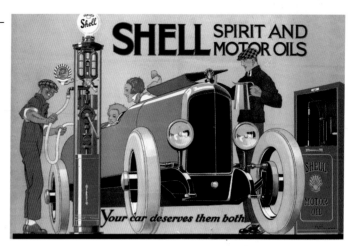

THE BIG SELL
Black and sticky, oil is not obviously attractive. So oil companies went out of their way to give their oil a glamorous image in order to maximize sales. Advertisements used bright colours and stylish locations, and some of the best young artists of the day were hired to create wonderful-looking posters. This one for Shell oils dates from 1926. The oil itself is nowhere to be seen.

In the absence of the real thing, some women even stained their legs to simulate the colour of nylons

Faking nylons, 1940s

NYLONS
In the 1930s, companies looked for ways to use the oil leftover after motor oil had been extracted. In 1935, Wallace Carothers of the DuPont™ chemical company used oil to create a strong, stretchy artificial fibre called Nylon. Launched in 1939, nylon stockings were an instant hit with young women. During the hardships of World War II (1939–45), when nylons were in short supply, women often faked nylons by drawing black "seams" down the backs of their legs.

Nylon stockings

Advertisement for Tupperware, 1950s

Advert portrays an idealized image of domestic life

EARLY PLASTICS
Many plastics familiar today had their origins in the oil boom, as scientists discovered they could make plastics such as PVC and polythene from oil. When prosperity returned after World War II, a vast range of cheap, everyday plastic products was introduced for use in the home. The most famous was polythene "Tupperware" food storage boxes, launched by DuPont™ chemist Earl Tupper in 1946.

What is oil?

OIL AND NATURAL GAS together make up petroleum, which is Latin for "rock oil". Petroleum is a dark, oily substance that is typically liquid, but it can also be solid or gaseous. When it comes straight out of the ground as a liquid it is called crude oil if it is dark and sticky, and condensate if clear and volatile (evaporates easily). When solid it is called asphalt, and when semi-solid it is called bitumen. Natural gas can be found either with oil or on its own. Petroleum is made entirely naturally, largely from the decomposed remains of living things. Although it looks like a simple gooey mass, it is actually a complex mixture of chemicals. Different chemical groups can be separated out at refineries and petrochemical plants, and then used to make a huge range of different substances.

Asphalt

STICKY STUFF
In some places, underground oil seeps up to the surface. Exposed to the air, its most volatile components evaporate to leave a black ooze or even a lump like this. When it is like thick treacle it is called bitumen; when it is like sticky toffee it is asphalt. These forms of oil are often referred to as pitch or tar.

NATURAL GAS
Oil contains some compounds that are so volatile that they evaporate easily and form natural gas. Nearly every oil deposit contains enough of these compounds to create at least some natural gas. Some deposits contain such a high proportion that they are virtually all gas.

Natural gas flame

Light oils float on water

Oil and water do not mix

LIGHT AND HEAVY OIL
Thin and volatile oils (crudes that readily evaporate) are described as "light", whereas thick and viscous oils (crudes that do not flow well) are said to be "heavy". Most oils float easily on water, but some heavy oils will actually sink (although not in sea water, which has a higher density than fresh water).

CRUDE OIL
Crude oil is usually thick and oily, but it can come in a huge range of compositions and colours, including black, green, red, or brown. Crude oil from Sudan is jet black and North Sea oil is dark brown. Oil from the US state of Utah is amber, while oil from parts of Texas is almost straw-coloured. "Sweet" crudes are oils that are easy to refine because they contain little sulphur. "Sour" oils contain more sulphur, and consequently need more processing.

Brown crude oil

Black crude oil

Hydrogen atom

Carbon atom

Octane hydrocarbon molecule

Aromatics 15%

Alkanes 60%

Naphthenes 25%

Saudi heavy crude

OIL MIXTURE
Oil mainly contains the elements hydrogen (14 per cent by weight) and carbon (84 per cent). These are combined in oil as chemical compounds called hydrocarbons. There are three main types of oil hydrocarbon, called alkanes, aromatics, and naphthenes. This diagram shows the approximate proportions of these substances in "Saudi heavy" crude oil, which is higher in alkanes than many crude oils.

HYDROCARBON CHEMICALS
The hydrocarbons in crude oil have either ring- or chain-shaped molecules. Alkanes, including methane and octane, have chain-like molecules. Aromatics, such as benzene, have ring molecules, while naphthenes are heavy-ring hydrocarbons. Oil also contains tiny amounts of non-hydrogen compounds called NSOs, which are mostly nitrogen, sulphur, and oxygen.

COW GAS

Methane, a constituent of oil, is a naturally abundant hydrocarbon. It is a simple hydrocarbon, with each molecule consisting of just a single carbon atom attached to four hydrogen atoms. Vast quantities of methane are locked up within organic material on the sea bed. The world's livestock also emit huge amounts of methane gas by flatulence. The methane forms as bacteria break down food in the animals' digestive systems.

PLANT HYDROCARBONS

Hydrocarbons occur naturally in many plant oils and animal fats, too. The smells of plants and flowers are produced by hydrocarbons known as essential oils. Perfume makers often heat, steam, or crush plants to extract these essential oils for use in their scents. Essential oils called terpenes are used as natural flavouring additives in food. Moth repellents contain a terpene called camphor that moths dislike.

Lavender's scent comes from a mix of terpene hydrocarbons

Lavender

This chain molecule is called octane because it is made from eight carbon and hydrogen groups

Each group consists of one carbon atom and two hydrogen atoms

Rice is a good source of starch

CARBOHYDRATES

People often confuse hydrocarbons and carbohydrates. Hydrocarbon molecules have a structure based on carbon and hydrogen atoms, but carbohydrates have oxygen built into their structure as well. The addition of oxygen enables them to take a huge variety of complex forms that are essential to living things. Carbohydrates such as starches and sugars are the basic energy foods of both plants and animals. Starches release energy more slowly than sugars.

Sugar cane is rich in sugars, which provide the body with instant energy

Babies could not be conceived without the hydrocarbon hormones in their parents' bodies

Bitumen — Fuel oil (for power stations and ships) — Heavy lubricating oil — Medium lubricating oil — Light lubricating oil — Diesel — Jet fuel (paraffin) — Petrol

HYDROCARBONS IN THE BODY

There are many natural hydrocarbons in the human body. One is cholesterol, the oily, fatty substance in your blood that helps to build the walls of blood vessels. Other crucial hydrocarbons in the body include the steroid hormones, such as progesterone and testosterone, which are very important in sex and reproduction.

SPLITTING OIL

Each of the hydrocarbons in crude oil has different properties. To make use of these properties, crude oil is refined (processed) to separate it into different groups of hydrocarbons, as seen above. The groups can be identified essentially by their density and viscosity, with bitumen being the most dense and viscous, and petrol the least.

Where oil comes from

SCIENTISTS ONCE THOUGHT THAT MOST OIL was formed by chemical reactions between minerals in rocks deep underground. Now, the majority of scientists believe that only a little oil was formed like this. Much of the world's oil formed, they think, from the remains of living things over a vast expanse of time. The theory is that the corpses of countless microscopic marine organisms, such as foraminifera and particularly plankton, piled up on the sea bed as a thick sludge, and were gradually buried deeper by sediments accumulating on top of them. There the remains were transformed over millions of years – first by bacteria and then by heat and pressure inside Earth – into liquid oil. The oil slowly seeped through the rocks and collected in underground pockets called traps, where it is tapped by oil wells today.

CONCENTRATED POWER SOURCE
Oil is packed with energy, stored in the bonds that hold its hydrocarbon molecules together. Ultimately, all this energy comes from the Sun. Long ago, tiny organisms called phytoplankton used energy from sunlight to convert simple chemicals into food in a process called photosynthesis. As the dead phytoplankton were changed into oil, this trapped energy became ever more concentrated.

Magnified view of diatoms

Diatoms have glassy shells made of silica

Light greeny-blue patches are phytoplankton blooms

Diatom shells come in many different shapes, and they are often complex, beautiful structures

BLOOMING OCEANS
The formation of oil probably relies on the huge growth of plankton that often occur in the shallow ocean waters off continents. Called blooms, they create thick masses of plant-like phytoplankton. The blooms can be so large that they are visible in satellite images like the one above, which shows the Bay of Biscay, France. Blooms typically erupt in spring, when sunshine and an upwelling of cold, nutrient-rich water from the depths provokes explosive plankton growth.

PLANKTON SOUP
The surface waters of oceans and lakes are rich in floating plankton. Although far too small to see with the naked eye, plankton are so abundant that their corpses form thick blankets on the sea bed. There are two main types of plankton. Phytoplankton, like plants, can make their own food using sunlight. Zooplankton feed on phytoplankton and on each other. The most abundant phytoplankton are called diatoms.

Tiny one-celled organisms called foraminifera, or "forams", are abundant throughout the world's oceans. Like diatoms, they are a prime source material for oil. Forams secrete a shell or casing around themselves called a test. Chalk rock is rich in fossilized foram shells. Every era and rock layer seemed to have its own special foram, so oil prospectors look for forams when drilling to gain an insight into the history of the rock.

Chalk cliffs containing fossilized foraminifera, Sussex, England

Microscopic foram shell with pores

Shell is made of calcium carbonate

HOW OIL FORMS
The buried marine organisms are first ̶otted by bacteria into substances called kerogen and bitumen. As kerogen and bitumen are buried deeper – between ̶,000 and 6,000 m (3,300 and 10,000 ft) – heat and pressure "cook" them. This turns them into bubbles of oil and natural gas. The bubbles are spread ̶throughout porous rock, like water in a ̶sponge. Over millions of years, some of them seep up through the rock, collecting in traps when they meet impermeable rock layers.

Marine organisms die and are buried underneath the sea floor

Microscopic view of kerogen particle

Oil and natural gas form in porous sedimentary rock

Oil and gas migrate upwards

Impermeable rock does not let oil or gas pass through

Trapped gas

Trapped oil

̶ALFWAY STAGE
̶st a small proportion of the ̶uried remains of microscopic ̶narine organisms turns into oil. ̶Most only undergoes the first ̶tage of transformation, into kerogen. This is a browny-black ̶olid found in sedimentary ̶ocks (those formed from the ̶ebris of other rocks and living ̶nings). To turn into oil, kerogen ̶ust be heated under pressure ̶ more than 60°C (140°F).

OIL IN SPACE
Could oil-like rings and chains of hydrocarbons form in space? After analyzing the colour of light from distant stars, astronomers believe that they might well do. Observations by the Infrared Space Observatory satellite of the dying star CRL618 in 2001 detected the presence of benzene, which has the classic ring-shaped hydrocarbon molecule.

Natural gas

THOUSANDS OF YEARS AGO, people in parts of Greece, Persia, and India noticed a gas seeping from the ground that caught fire very easily. These natural gas flames sometimes became the focus of myths or religious beliefs. Natural gas is a mixture of gases, but it contains mostly methane – the smallest and lightest hydrocarbon. Like oil, natural gas formed underground from the remains of tiny marine organisms, and it is often brought up at the same wells as crude oil. It can also come from wells that contain only gas and condensate, or from "natural" wells that provide natural gas alone. Little use was made of natural gas until fairly recently. In the early 20th century, oil wells burned it off as waste. Today, natural gas is a valued fuel that supplies over a quarter of the world's energy.

WILL-O'-THE-WISP
When organic matter rots, it may release a gas (now called biogas) that is a mixture of methane and phosphine. Bubbles of biogas seeping from marshes and briefly catching fire gave birth to the legend of the "will-o'-the-wisp" – ghostly lights said be used by spirits or demons to lure travellers to their doom, as seen here.

Worker inspecting a natural gas pipe, Russia

PIPING GAS
Most natural gas brought up from underground is transported by pipeline. Major gas pipelines are assembled from sections of carbon steel, each rigorously tested for pressure resistance. Gas is pumped through the pipes under immense pressure. The pressure not only reduces the volume of the gas to be transported by up to 600 times, but it also provides the "push" to move the gas through the pipe.

EXTRACTION AND PROCESSING
Natural gas is often extracted at plants like the one below. The gas is so light that it rises up the gas well without any need for pumping. Before being piped away for use, it has to be processed to remove impurities and unwanted elements. "Sour gas", which is high in sulphur and carbon dioxide, is highly corrosive and dangerous, so it needs extra processing. Because processed natural gas has no smell, substances called thiols are added to give it a distinct odour so that leaks can be detected.

A typical LNG tanker holds more than 150 million litres (33 million gallons) of LNG, with an energy content equivalent to 91 billion litres (20 billion gallons) of the gaseous form

Burning flame indicates gas is flowing

Extraction and processing plant at gas field near Noviy Urengoy, western Siberia, Russia

Gas lamps had to be lit individually each night

STREET REVOLUTION

The introduction of gas street lamps to London in the early years of the 19th century marked the beginning of a revolution. Before long, city streets the world over – once almost totally dark at night – were filled with bright, instant light. Although natural gas was used for street lighting as early as 1816, most 19th-century street lamps burned a gas known as coal gas, which was manufactured from coal. Electricity began to replace gas for street lighting during the early part of the 20th century.

TOWN GAS

By the mid-18th century, most towns had their own gas works for making coal gas, or "town gas" as it was also known. The gas was stored in vast metal tanks called gasometers, which became familiar sights in urban areas. In addition to lighting, town gas had many other uses, including cooking and heating. Town gas fell out of use in the second half of the 20th century, after the discovery of vast natural gas fields and the building of pipelines had made natural gas more widely available. Natural gas was also cheaper and safer to use than town gas.

Gasometers sank into the ground as the level of gas inside went down

Heavily reinforced tanks keep the gas pressurized and in liquid form

A single tank contains enough energy to meet all the USA's electricity needs for five minutes

GAS TANKER

Not all gas travels through pipelines – especially when it has to go to far-off destinations overseas. Huge ships equipped with spherical storage tanks carry gas across the ocean in a form called liquid natural gas, or LNG. This is made by cooling natural gas to –160°C (–260°F). At that temperature, natural gas becomes liquid. As a liquid, its volume is less than 1/600th of its volume as a gas.

GAS CAVE

Natural gas is too bulky and flammable to store in tanks. After being processed and piped to its destination, the gas is stored underground ready for use, sometimes in old salt mines like this one in Italy. Other subterranean storage sites include aquifers (rock formations that hold water) and depleted gas reservoirs (porous rock that once held "raw" natural gas).

Processing units clean the gas of impurities and unwanted substances

Processed natural gas is pumped into pipes for distribution

Propane burns with a blue flame

GAS SPIN-OFFS

Gases such as ethane, propane, butane, and isobutane are removed from natural gas during processing. Most of these gases are sold separately. Propane and butane, for example, are sold in canisters as fuel for camping stoves. A few gas wells also contain helium. Best known for its use in balloons, helium also acts as a coolant in a range of devices, from nuclear reactors to body scanners.

Coal and peat

OIL AND NATURAL GAS are called "fossil" fuels because they are formed from the remains of long-dead living organisms, just like the fossils found in rocks. Coal is the third major fossil fuel. Peat is another, but it is only used in a small way. Coal was the power behind the Industrial Revolution in 19th-century Europe and America, fuelling the steam engines that drove factories and pulled trains. It provided heat for the home, too, in the fast-growing cities of that time. Coal's position as the number one fuel for transport has now been surpassed by oil, and for heat by natural gas, but it remains the main fuel used for generating electricity. It is also vital in making steel.

A FOREST OF COAL
Most of the coal in Europe, North America, and northern Asia originated in the Carboniferous and the Permian eras, some 300 million years ago. At that time, these continents lay mostly in the tropics. Vast areas were covered with steamy swamps, where giant club mosses and tree ferns grew in profusion.

Plant matter

Peat

Lignite (brown coal)

Bituminous coal

Anthracite

Increasing depth and heat

1. When swamp plants died their remains rotted slowly in stagnant water

2. Gradually, more and more remains piled up, squeezing lower layers dry and turning them into a soft mass called peat

3. Over millions of years, the peat was buried more than 4 km (2.5 miles) deep, where it began to cook in the heat of Earth's interior

Layer or "seam" of coal

4. Cooking destroyed the remaining plant fibre and drove out gases, leaving mainly solid black carbon

HOW COAL FORMED
Oil and natural gas formed from tiny marine organisms, but coal formed from the remains of vegetation that grew in tropical swamps. As the forests died and were buried under layers of swamp mud, they were slowly altered by pressure and heat. This squeezed the plant remains dry and hardened them, and also drove out hydrogen, sulphur, and other gases to leave solid carbon.

COOKED INTO CARBON
The deeper and longer plant debris is buried and the hotter it gets, the more it turns to carbon and the better fuel it produces. Peat forms quickly near the surface. Soft, moist, and brown, it is only 60 per cent carbon. Brown lignite coal forms deeper than peat and is 73 per cent carbon. The blacker bituminous coal forms even deeper still, and is 85 per cent carbon. Black anthracite, the deepest coal, is over 90 per cent carbon.

COAL FROM THE SURFACE
The way companies mine coal depends partly on how deep the coal is buried. When it is less than 100 m (330 ft) below the surface, the cheapest method is to simply strip off the overlying material with a giant shovel called a dragline, and then dig out the coal. Lignite tends to occur near the surface, and can often be mined economically by such "strip mining". But it would not be worth mining such low-quality coal from deep underground.

COAL FROM DEEP DOWN
The best bituminous and anthracite coal typically lies in narrow layers called seams, far below ground. To get at the coal, mining companies first sink a deep shaft. Then they create a maze of horizontal or gently sloping tunnels to get into the seam, and extract the coal using specially designed coal-cutting machinery. The surface of the exposed seam is called the coal face.

WASHING WITH COAL
When coal is baked in a kiln it turns to a very dry, ash-free solid called coke, which is burned to heat iron ore in steel-making processes. One of the by-products of coke production is coal gas, which was widely used in the 19th century for lighting. Another by-product is a sticky liquid called coal tar. Once used to make soap, it is now the basis for dyes and paints.

Advertisement for coal tar soap, early 20th century

Fossilized fern in coal

The fern leaf's outline is perfectly preserved in almost pure carbon

FERN IMPRINT
Coal beds are excellent places to find fossils. Even huge fossilized tree trunks have been found in association with coal beds. In fact, the character of the coal itself depends largely on which part of the plant it was mostly formed from. A tough coal called vitrain, for example, is high in a material called vitrinite, which is made from the plant's woody parts.

FOR PEAT'S SAKE
Peat forms best when there is little oxygen around, which is why the warm, stagnant swamps of long ago produced so much of it. But this old peat eventually turned to coal. Most peat found today was formed fairly recently in cold bogs. Some power stations in Ireland burn peat, but this is controversial because peat bogs are important natural habitats.

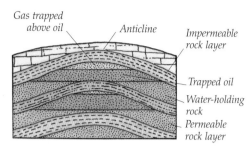

Gas trapped above oil — Anticline — Impermeable rock layer — Trapped oil — Water-holding rock — Permeable rock layer

ANTICLINE TRAP
Oil is often trapped under anticlines – places where layers (strata) of rock have been bent up into an arch by the movement of Earth's crust. If one of these bent layers is impermeable, the oil may ooze up underneath it and accumulate there. Anticline traps like this hold much of the world's oil.

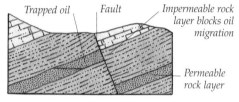

Trapped oil — Fault — Impermeable rock layer blocks oil migration — Permeable rock layer

FAULT TRAP
Every now and then, rock strata crack and slide up or down past each other. This is known as a fault. Faults can create oil traps in various ways. The most common is when the fault slides a layer of impermeable rock across a layer of permeable rock through which oil is migrating.

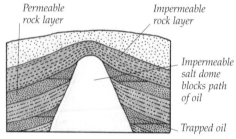

Permeable rock layer — Impermeable rock layer — Impermeable salt dome blocks path of oil — Trapped oil

SALT-DOME TRAP
When masses of salt form deep underground, heat and pressure cause them to bulge upward in domes. The rising domes force the overlying rock layers aside. As they do so, they can cut across layers of permeable rock, blocking the path of any migrating oil and creating an oil trap.

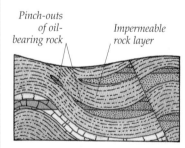

Pinch-outs of oil-bearing rock — Impermeable rock layer

PINCH-OUT TRAPS
Anticline, fault, and salt-dome traps are created by the arrangement of the rock layers, and are called structural traps. Stratigraphic traps are created by variations within the rock layers themselves. A pinch-out is a common type of stratigraphic trap. Pinch-out traps are often formed from old stream beds, where a lens-shaped region of permeable sand becomes trapped within less permeable shales and siltstones.

Oil traps

W HEN OIL COMPANIES DRILL FOR OIL, they look for oil traps. These are places where oil collects underground after seeping up through the surrounding rocks. This slow seepage, called migration, begins soon after liquid oil first forms in a "source" rock. Shales, rich in solid organic matter known as kerogen, are the most common type of source rock. The oil forms when the kerogen is altered by heat and pressure deep underground. As source rocks become buried ever deeper over time, oil and gas may be squeezed out like water from a sponge and migrate through permeable rocks. These are rocks with tiny cracks through which fluids can seep. The oil is frequently mixed with water and, since oil floats on water, the oil tends to migrate upwards. Sometimes, though, it comes up against impermeable rock, through which it cannot pass. Then it becomes trapped and slowly accumulates, forming a reservoir.

ROCK BENDS
It seems amazing that layers of solid rock can be bent, but the movement of the huge rock plates that make up Earth's crust (outer layer) generates incredible pressures. The layers of sedimentary rock exposed here in this road cutting originally formed flat from sediments deposited on the sea bed. The dramatic arch, or anticline, was created as giant slabs of crust moved relentlessly together, crumpling the rock layers between. Countless anticline arches like this around the world become traps for oil.

Rock strata (layers)

RESERVOIR ROCKS

The oil created in source rocks only becomes accessible once it has migrated to rocks that have plenty of pores and cracks for oil to move through and accumulate in. Rocks where oil accumulates are called reservoir rocks. Most reservoir rocks, such as sandstone and to a lesser extent limestone and dolomite, have fairly large grains. The grains are loosely packed, allowing oil to seep between them.

Sandstone

Anticline dome

Pea-sized grains

Pisolitic limestone

Dolomite

VIEW FROM ABOVE

Anticlines often form long domes that are visible as ovals on geological maps or in satellite photographs. Here a satellite photograph reveals a series of oval anticline domes in the Zagros mountains of southwestern Iran. Each dome forms a separate, tapering mini-mountain range, looking from above like a giant half melon. Such domes would be prime targets for oil prospectors looking for major oil deposits, and the Zagros mountains are indeed one of the world's oldest and richest oil fields.

TRAP ROCK

Oil will go on migrating through permeable rocks until its path is blocked by impermeable rocks – rocks in which the pores are too small or the cracks too narrow or too disconnected for oil or water to seep through. Where impermeable rock seals oil into a trap, it is called trap rock (or cap rock). The trap rock acts like the lid on the oil reservoir. The most common trap rock is shale.

Ultra-fine grains packed tightly together

Shale

Anticline (arch-shaped upfold)

Rock darkened by the organic content from which oil can form

Each rock type is shown in a particular colour

William Smith
(1769–1839)

Detail from Smith's geological map of England and Wales, 1815

SMITH'S LAYERS

The knowledge of rock layers so crucial to the search for oil began with William Smith, an English canal engineer who made the first geological maps. As Smith was surveying routes for canals, he noticed that different rock layers contained particular fossils. He realized that if layers some distance apart had the same fossils, then they must be the same age. This enabled him to trace rock layers right across the landscape, and understand how they had been folded and faulted.

Solid oil

MOST OF THE OIL THE WORLD USES is black, liquid crude oil drawn up from subterranean pools. Yet this is just a tiny fraction of the oil that lies below ground. A vast quantity of more solid oil exists underground in the form of oil sands and oil shales. Oil sands (once known as tar sands) are sand and clay deposits in which each grain is covered by sticky bitumen oil. Oil shales are rocks steeped in kerogen – the organic material that turns to liquid oil when cooked under pressure. Extracting oil from oil shales and oil sands involves heating them so that the oil drains out. At the moment, this is not really economical, but many experts believe that when crude oil reserves begin to run out, oil shales and oil sands may become our main sources of oil.

MUCKY SAND
Oil sands look like black, very sticky mud. Each grain of sand is covered by a film of water surrounded by a "slick" of bitumen. In winter, the water freezes, making the sand as hard as concrete. In summer, when the water melts, the sand becomes treacly.

ATHABASCA OIL SANDS
Oil sands are found in many places around the world, but the world's largest deposits are in Alberta, Canada, and in Venezuela, which each have about a third of the world's oil sands. Alberta, though, is the only place where the oil sands are extracted in any quantity, because the deposit at Athabasca (representing 10 per cent of Alberta's oil sands) is the only one near enough to the surface to be dug out economically.

These trucks are the biggest in the world, each weighing 400 tonnes

Each truck carries 400 tonnes of sandy bitumen, the equivalent of 200 barrels of crude oil

EXTRACTION TECHNIQUES
If oil sands are near the surface, they are mined by digging a huge pit. Giant trucks carry the sand to a large machine that breaks up the lumps in the sand, then mixes it with hot water to make a slurry. The slurry is sent by pipeline to a separation plant, where the oil is removed from the sand for processing at a refinery. However, if the sands are too deep to dig out, oil companies may try to extract just the oil by injecting steam. The steam melts the bitumen and helps to separate it from the sand. It is then pumped to the surface and sent off for processing. Another method is to inject oxygen to start a fire and melt the oil. These techniques are still experimental.

Fossilized
Smilodon skull

STICKY END

Tar pits, or more correctly asphalt pits, are hollows where slightly runny asphalt seeps up through the ground to create a sticky black pool. Remarkably complete fossils of prehistoric *Smilodon*s (sabre-tooths) and their mammoth prey have been found together in tar pits, such as the famous La Brea pit in California, USA. It seems that the mammoths got stuck in the pool and the *Smilodon*s, pursuing their prey, followed them in and became stuck too.

Smilodon *is sometimes known as "sabre-tooth" because of its pair of sabre-like teeth, which were used for ripping flesh*

*Smilodon*s maul a mammoth in a tar pit

Pitch Lake, Trinidad

PITCHING IN

Trinidad's Pitch Lake is a huge natural lake of asphalt thought to be 75 m (250 ft) deep. The lake is believed to be above the intersection of two faults (cracks in the rock bed), through which the asphalt oozes up from deep underground. The English explorer Sir Walter Raleigh spotted the lake on his travels to the Caribbean in 1595, and used its asphalt to waterproof his ships for his homeward journey.

Sir Walter
Raleigh (1552–1618)

OILY ROADS

The Ancient Babylonians used bitumen to make smooth, waterproof roads 2,500 ago. Modern road surfaces date from the early 19th century, when road builders began making roads with gravel bound together by hot coal tar or bitumen. The material was called tarmacadam, or tarmac, because the tar was added to a mix of graded gravel devised by John Loudon McAdam (1756–1836), a Scottish road engineer.

SCOTTISH OIL

The modern oil industry began in Scotland in 1848, when James Young (1811–83) found a way of producing paraffin for lamps using oil taken from seeps. Oil seeps were rare in Britain, so Young turned to an oil shale found in the Scottish lowlands called cannel coal, or torbanite. In 1851, he set up the world's first oil refinery at Bathgate near Edinburgh to distil oil from torbanite mined nearby.

Oil shales are turned black by kerogen held in pores in the rock

Marlstone, a type of oil shale

OIL SHALE

Although there are vast deposits of oil shale, notably in Colorado, USA, it is hard to extract oil from them. The kerogen has to be melted out and then turned into oil by intense heat in a process called retorting. The rock can be mined and retorted on the surface, but this is expensive. Engineers think that in the future it may be possible to melt the oil out using electric heaters inserted into the rock.

How oil is found

Truck with recording equipment

Geophones detect reflected waves

Explosion

Limestone

Seismic waves reflect off the limestone layer

OIL SHAKES
Seismic surveys send powerful vibrations, or seismic waves, through the ground from an explosion or a sound generator. Surveyors record how the waves reflect back to the surface off subterranean rocks. Different rock types reflect seismic waves differently, so surveyors can build up a detailed picture of the rock structure from the pattern of reflections.

IN THE PAST, finding oil except close to where it seeped visibly to the surface was largely a matter of guesswork and sheer luck. Nowadays, oil prospectors use their knowledge of the way geology creates oil traps to guide them to areas where oil is likely to occur. They know, for example, that oil is likely to be found in one of the 600 or so basins of sedimentary rock around the world, and it is in these basins that oil exploration tends to be concentrated. So far, about 160 basins have yielded oil, and 240 have drawn a blank. Hunting for oil within sedimentary basins might begin by examining exposed rock outcrops for likely looking formations, or scanning satellite and radar images. Once a target area has been located, oil hunters carry out geophysical surveys that use sophisticated equipment to detect subtle clues such as variations in Earth's magnetic and gravitational fields created by the presence of oil.

COMPUTER MODELLING
The most sophisticated seismic surveys use numerous probes to survey the deep structures in a particular area. The results are then fed into a computer and used to build up a detailed 3-D model, known as a volume, of underground rock formations. Such 3-D models are expensive to generate, but drilling a well in the wrong place can waste millions of pounds.

Computer-model of rock formations

Hydraulic pads send vibrations through ground

Soft tyres for travel over rough terrain

Weights to keep truck balanced

HUNTING UNDER THE SEA
Seismic surveys can also be used to hunt for oil under the sea bed. Boats tow cables attached to sound detectors called hydrophones. In the past, the vibrations were made by dynamite explosions, but this killed too many sea creatures. Now the vibrations are set off by releasing bubbles of compressed air, which send out sound waves as they expand and contract while rising to the surface.

THUMPING TRUCKS
With seismic surveys on land, the vibrations are set off either by small explosive charges in the ground or by special trucks. These trucks, which are known as vibes, have a hydraulic pad that shakes the ground with tremendous force, at a rate of 5 to 80 times per second. The vibrations, which are clearly audible, penetrate deep into the ground. They reflect back to the surface and are picked up by detectors called geophones.

MAGNETIC SEARCH
Magnetic searches are usually conducted using an aircraft like this, which is equipped with a device called a magnetometer. The magnetometer detects variations in the magnetism of the ground below. The sedimentary rocks where oil is likely to be found are generally much less magnetic than rocks that form volcanically, which are rich in magnetic metals such as iron and nickel.

Drill begins, or "spuds in", a new well

TEST DRILL
In the past, "wildcat" wells were drilled in places where the oil hunters had little more than a hunch that oil might be found. Today, test drilling is carried out in locations where the results of surveying suggest that there is a reasonable likelihood of an oil strike. Even so, the chances of finding quantities of oil or gas that can be commercially exploited are less than 1 in 5.

Screws to adjust spring tension

Inside a gravimeter is a weight suspended from springs

Screen shows slight variations in the stretching of the springs caused by gravitational differences

BORE SAMPLE
Drilling is the only way to be sure that an oil or gas field exists, and exactly what kind of oil is present. Once a test drill has been bored, the oil prospectors use downhole logging equipment, which detects the physical and chemical nature of the rocks. Rock samples are brought to the surface for detailed analysis in the laboratory.

USING GRAVITY
Rocks of different densities have a slightly different gravitational pull. Gravity meters, or gravimeters, can measure these minute differences at the surface using a weight suspended from springs. They can detect variations as small as one part in 10 million. These differences reveal features such as salt domes and masses of dense rock underground, helping geologists to build up a complete picture of the subsurface rock structure.

Getting the oil out

LOCATING A SUITABLE SITE for drilling is just the first step in extracting oil. Before drilling can begin, companies must make sure that they have the legal right to drill, and that the impact of drilling on the environment is acceptable. This can take years. Once they finally have the go ahead, drilling begins. The exact procedure varies, but the idea is first to drill down to just above where the oil is located. Then they insert a casing of concrete into the newly drilled hole to make it stronger. Next, they make little holes in the casing near the bottom, which will let oil in, and top the well with a special assembly of control- and safety-valves called a "Christmas tree". Finally, they may send down acid or pressurized sand to break through the last layer of rock and start the oil flowing into the well.

BLOW-OUTS AND GUSHERS
Oil underground is often under high pressure. If a well's safety valves are not properly fitted, suddenly bursting through to the oil can cause a blow-out. This is an uncontrolled release of a mixture of oil, gas, sand, mud, and water, which can race up the bore at near-supersonic speeds. It may shoot into the air as a gusher up to 60 m (200 ft) high.

WELL DRILLED
Virtually all you see of an oil well on the surface is the drilling rig – a platform with a tower called a derrick that supports the drill. The rig also has generators to provide power, pumps to circulate a special fluid called drilling mud, and mechanisms to hoist and turn the drill. The bore (drill hole) beneath the rig can be thousands of metres deep. When the drillers near the final depth, they remove the drill and perform tests to ensure that it is safe to proceed. They also conduct wireline-logging tests, which involve lowering electrical sensors to assess the rock formations at the bottom of the bore. After all the tests have been satisfactorily completed, the oil can be extracted.

STRING AND MUD
Drilling thousands of metres into solid rock is a tricky business. Unlike a hand-drill, an oil drill does not have a single drilling rod, but a long "string" made from hundreds of pieces, added on one by one as the drill goes deeper. Drilling mud is pumped continuously around the drill to minimize friction. The mud also cools and cleans the drill bit, and carries the "cuttings" (drilled rock fragments) back up to the surface.

Derrick

Swivel mechanism allows drill string to turn

Hose feeds drilling mud into the bore

Electricity generators

Mud return pipe

Mud pump

Mud pit

Rock strata

Drill string

Concrete casing

Drill collar

Drill bit

Mud is pumped down inside the drill string

The mud travels back up the casing of the bore, taking rock cuttings with it

DIAMOND TEETH
Right at the bottom end of the string is the drill bit, which turns continuously and cuts slowly into the rock. Different rocks call for different designs of drill bit. The cutting edges of the teeth are toughened with different combinations of steel, tungsten-carbide, diamond, or PDC (synthetic diamond), according to the type of rock to be drilled.

Nozzle sprays mud on to the drill bit

*Fire is fed by
pressurized oil
and gas*

*Screen protects
firefighters as they
tackle the blaze*

RED ADAIR
Paul Neal "Red" Adair (1915–2004)
was world-renowned for his exploits
in fighting oil-well fires. The Texan's
most famous feat was tackling a fire
in the Sahara Desert in 1962, an
exploit retold in the John Wayne
movie *Hellfighters* (1968). When oil
wells in Kuwait caught fire during the
Gulf War of 1991, it was the veteran
Red Adair, then aged 77, who was
called in to put them out.

FIRE FOUNTAIN
The force of a blow-out can
be so great that it wrecks the
drilling rig. Improved drilling
techniques have made blow-
outs much rarer than they used
to be, but they still occur from
time to time. If the blow-out
ignites, it burns fiercely, and the
fire is difficult to extinguish.
Fortunately, there are now only
a handful of blow-out fires
around the world each year.

WELL-CAPPING
Sometimes, the drilling crew loses control of
the flow of oil and gas and is faced with
a blow-out. If this happens, they must
cap the well as quickly as possible.
To do this, they use a special valve
called a blow-out preventer, or
BOP. The BOP allows them to
close off the well and release
the pressure slowly. Thanks
to BOPs, gushers are
now largely a thing
of the past.

Offshore oil rigs

SOMETIMES LARGE RESERVES OF OIL are found deep beneath the ocean bed. To get the oil out, huge drilling rigs are built far out at sea to provide a platform for drills that bore right down into the rocks of the sea floor. The oil is sent ashore via pipelines or held in separate floating storage facilities before being off-loaded into large tankers. Offshore oil rigs are gigantic structures. Many have legs that stretch hundreds of metres from the surface to the ocean floor. The Petronius Platform in the Gulf of Mexico, for example, is the world's tallest structure, standing some 610 m (2,000 ft) above the sea bed. Rigs have to be immensely strong, able to withstand gale-force winds and relentless pounding by huge waves.

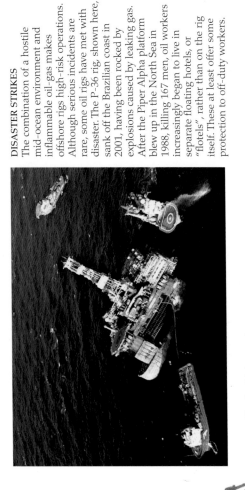

DISASTER STRIKES

The combination of a hostile mid-ocean environment and inflammable oil-gas makes offshore rigs high-risk operations. Although serious incidents are rare, some oil rigs have met with disaster. The P-36 rig, shown here, sank off the Brazilian coast in 2001, having been rocked by explosions caused by leaking gas. After the Piper Alpha platform blew up in the North Sea in 1988, killing 167 men, oil workers increasingly began to live in separate floating hotels, or "flotels", rather than on the rig itself. These at least offer some protection to off-duty workers.

Any gas that rises with the oil and cannot be used is burned off, or "flared", as a safety precaution

Helicopters carry workers to and from the rig

Landing pad

Fireproof lifeboats

The derrick is a steel tower that contains the drilling equipment

The drill cable, or "string", is made from lengths of steel pipe 10 m (33 ft) long. The drill bit is attached to the end

Cranes hoist supplies from ships up to the platform

RIGOROUS MAINTENANCE

Any fault in the structure of an oil rig – such as parts that have come loose or been weakened by rust – could spell disaster. The rig's engineers must maintain their vigilance round the clock, checking the structure over and over again for any signs of problems. Here they are being lowered from the platform to inspect the rig's legs for cracks after a heavy storm.

In the event of a fire, fireboats can spray thousands of litres of water per minute at the flames

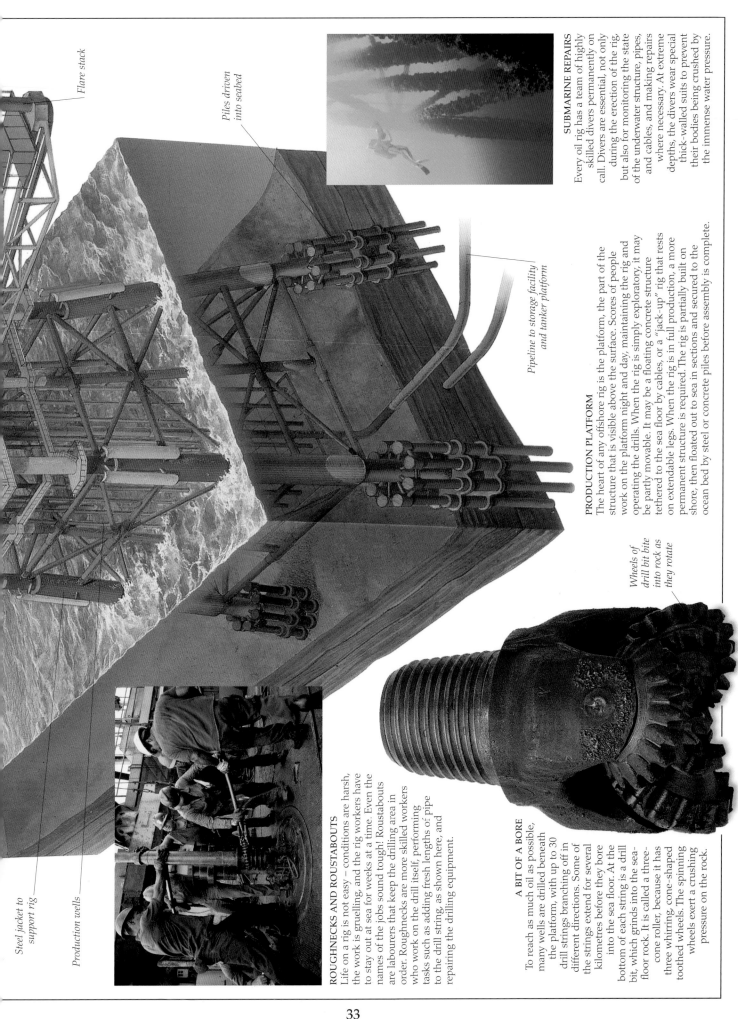

Flare stack

Piles driven into seabed

Steel jacket to support rig

Production wells

Pipeline to storage facility and tanker platform

Wheels of drill bit bite into rock as they rotate

SUBMARINE REPAIRS

Every oil rig has a team of highly skilled divers permanently on call. Divers are essential, not only during the erection of the rig, but also for monitoring the state of the underwater structure, pipes, and cables, and making repairs where necessary. At extreme depths, the divers wear special thick-walled suits to prevent their bodies being crushed by the immense water pressure.

PRODUCTION PLATFORM

The heart of any offshore rig is the platform, the part of the structure that is visible above the surface. Scores of people work on the platform night and day, maintaining the rig and operating the drills. When the rig is simply exploratory, it may be partly movable. It may be a floating concrete structure tethered to the sea floor by cables, or a "jack-up" rig that rests on extendable legs. When the rig is in full production, a more permanent structure is required. The rig is partially built on shore, then floated out to sea in sections and secured to the ocean bed by steel or concrete piles before assembly is complete.

ROUGHNECKS AND ROUSTABOUTS

Life on a rig is not easy – conditions are harsh, the work is gruelling, and the rig workers have to stay out at sea for weeks at a time. Even the names of the jobs sound tough! Roustabouts are labourers that keep the drilling area in order. Roughnecks are more skilled workers who work on the drill itself, performing tasks such as adding fresh lengths of pipe to the drill string, as shown here, and repairing the drilling equipment.

A BIT OF A BORE

To reach as much oil as possible, many wells are drilled beneath the platform, with up to 30 drill strings branching off in different directions. Some of the strings extend for several kilometres before they bore into the sea floor. At the bottom of each string is a drill bit, which grinds into the sea-floor rock. It is called a three-cone roller, because it has three whirring, cone-shaped toothed wheels. The spinning wheels exert a crushing pressure on the rock.

33

Piped oil

IN THE EARLY DAYS OF THE OIL INDUSTRY, oil was carted laboriously away from oil wells in wooden barrels. The oil companies soon realized that the best way to move oil was to pump it through pipes. Today there are vast networks of pipelines around the world, both on land and under the sea. The USA alone has about 305,000 km (190,000 miles) of oil pipes. The pipelines carry an array of different oil products, from petrol to jet fuel, sometimes in "batches" within the same pipe separated by special plugs. Largest of all are the "trunk" pipelines that take crude oil from drilling regions to refineries or ports. Some are up to 122 cm (48 in) in diameter and over 1,600 km (1,000 miles) long. Trunk lines are fed by smaller "gathering" lines that carry oil from individual wells.

PIPELINE CONSTRUCTION
Building an oil pipeline involves joining up tens of thousands of sections of steel piping. Each joint has to be expertly welded to prevent leakage. Construction is often relatively quick, since all the sections are prefabricated, but planning the pipeline's route and getting the agreement of all the people affected by it can take many years.

CLEVER PIGS
Every pipeline contains mobile plugs called pigs that travel along with the oil, either to separate batches of different oil products or to check for problems. The pigs get their name because early models made squealing noises as they moved through the pipes. A "smart" pig is a robot inspection unit with a sophisticated array of sensors. Propelled by the oil, the smart pig glides for hundreds of kilometres, monitoring every square centimetre of the pipe for defects such as corrosion.

OIL ON TAP
Completed in 1977, the Trans-Alaska Pipeline System (TAPS) stretches for over 1,280 km (800 miles) across Alaska. It carries crude oil from producer regions in the north to the port of Valdez in the south, from where the oil is shipped around the world. Arctic conditions and the need to cross mountain ranges and large rivers presented huge challenges to the construction engineers. Most US pipelines are subterranean, but much of the TAPS had to be built above ground because the soil in parts of Alaska is always frozen.

Aerogel is such a good insulator that just a thin layer is enough to block the heat of this flame and stop the matches catching fire

KEEPING IT WARM
If oil gets too cold, it becomes thicker and more difficult to pump through pipelines. Because of this, many pipes in colder parts of the world and under the sea are insulated with "aerogel". Created from a sponge-like jelly of silica and carbon, aerogel is the world's lightest material, made of 99 per cent air. All this air makes aerogel a remarkably good insulator.

THE POLITICS OF PIPELINE ROUTES
European nations wanted access to the Caspian Sea oil fields to make them less dependent on Russia and Iran for oil. So they backed the building of the Baku–Tbilisi–Ceyhan (BTC) pipeline. This runs 1,776 km (1,104 miles) from the Caspian Sea in Azerbaijan to the Mediterranean coast of Turkey via Georgia. Here the leaders of Georgia, Azerbaijan, and Turkey pose at the pipeline's completion in 2006.

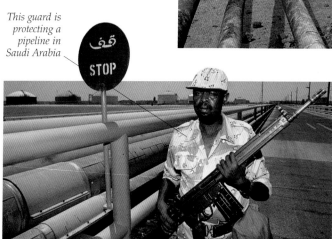

QUAKE RISK
Scientists constantly monitor the ground for earth tremors along some parts of oil pipelines, since a strong earthquake could crack or break the pipes. This pipe was bent in a quake at Parkfield, California, USA, which sits on the famous San Andreas Fault, where two plates of Earth's crust slide past one another.

This guard is protecting a pipeline in Saudi Arabia

قف
STOP

PIPELINES AND PEOPLE
Some pipelines are built through poor and environmentally sensitive regions, as seen here in Sumatra, Indonesia. Poor people living alongside the pipeline have no access to the riches carried by the pipe, but their lives can be disrupted by the construction – and any leaks once the pipeline is in operation. In some places, hundreds of local people have been killed by explosions caused by leaking pipes.

TERRORIST THREAT
Oil supplies carried by pipelines are so vital that they may become targets for terrorists, especially since many pass through politically unstable areas, such as parts of the Middle East. To guard against this threat, oil pipelines in some places are watched continuously by armed guards. However, many pipelines are too vast to patrol along their entire length.

Oil on the ocean

The tanker's small crew mostly live and work in the deck house at the rear

DAY AND NIGHT, some 3,500 oil tankers ply the world's oceans, transporting oil to wherever it is wanted. Mostly they transport crude oil, but sometimes they carry refined products, and these need special handling – bitumen, for example, must be heated to over 120°C (250°F) for loading. The quantity of oil moved by the tankers is vast. Each day, some 30 million barrels of oil is on the move. That's one-and-a-half times the daily consumption of oil in the entire USA, and 15 times as much oil as is used in a day in the UK. To get a picture of just what a huge volume of liquid this is, imagine 2,000 Olympic swimming pools full to the brim with black oil. Modern double-hulled tanker designs and navigation systems mean that most of this oil is carried across the ocean safely. But every now and then there is an accident, and oil spills into the sea. Only a tiny fraction of all the oil transported is spilled, but the consequences can be devastating.

SUPERTANKER
The largest oil tankers, known as supertankers, are by far the world's biggest ships. They typically weigh over 300,000 tonnes empty and can carry millions of barrels of oil, worth hundreds of millions of pounds. Amazingly, these monster ships are so automated that they only need a crew of about 30. The vast size of supertankers means that they can take 10 km (6 miles) to stop, and they need up to 4 km (2.5 miles) to turn. In the oil trade, supertankers are called Ultra Large Crude Carriers (ULCCs). Very Large Crude Carriers (VLCCs) are not quite so large, but these tankers still weigh more than 200,000 tonnes.

FIRST AFLOAT
Back in 1861, the American sailing ship *Elizabeth Watts* carried 240 kegs of oil from Philadelphia to England. But carrying such a flammable substance in wooden kegs in a wooden ship was a hazardous business. Then in 1884, British shipbuilders purpose-built the steel-hulled steamship *Glückauf* (right), which held the oil in a steel tank. This was the first modern oil tanker.

The interior of the hull is divided into several separate tanks to minimize the amount of oil lost if the hull is pierced

Supertanker   Tug boat   Ocean liner

GIANTS OF THE OCEAN
Supertankers are gigantic vessels, easily dwarfing the largest ocean liners. Some are even longer than the Empire State Building laid on its side. The largest of all is the *Knock Nevis* (once called the *Jahre Viking*). At 458.4 m (1,503 ft 5 in) long, it is the biggest ship that ever took to the ocean. The *Knock Nevis* weighs 544,763 tonnes empty, and 825, 614 tonnes when fully laden.

The bulk of the cargo of oil is carried below the waterline for stability

On-shore storage tanks

OIL TERMINAL
After its long sea voyage, a tanker arrives at an oil terminal. Supertankers need water at least 20 m (66 ft) deep, so there is a limited number of suitable sites for oil terminals. The piers where the tankers moor are sometimes built so far out from the shore that dockers and crews have to drive to and from the ship. In future, some terminals may be built as artificial "sea islands" in deep water, from which oil is piped ashore.

Articulated-arm discharge system

Arm connects to manifold (oil outlet) on top of tanker

PUMPING OIL
To get oil off the tanker, long, articulated (jointed) arms swing into place. The arms are computer-controlled to enable them to hook up exactly with the oil outlet on the tanker's deck, known as the manifold. All the ship's oil tanks are connected to the manifold via valves and pipes. Once the arms are securely connected to the manifold, a pump called a deepwell cargo pump begins to pump the oil out.

Ballast tanks are empty when sailing under load

When sailing empty, the tanker takes on about 95,000 tonnes of sea water as ballast

A 300,000-tonne tanker has seven or eight cargo tanks for crude oil

Sailing under load

Sailing empty

DOUBLE HULLS FOR DOUBLE SAFETY
All large new tankers are now required by law to have a double hull, with a second hull inside the outer hull to give extra security against oil leaks if the ship is damaged. The 2–3 m (6–10 ft) gap between the hulls can also be filled with water to make up for the vast drop in weight (and stability) when the tanker is sailing empty of oil.

Plumage clogged with oil

BLACK PERIL
As well as oil spilled by tankers, oil may seep naturally into the ocean from the sea bed. But whatever the source, oil can do tremendous damage to marine life. Seabirds are especially vulnerable. Oil causes a bird's feathers to become matted so that they no longer keep out water or the cold. It can also cause the bird to lose buoyancy so that it drowns. When a bird tries to clean its feathers, it can be poisoned by the oil it swallows.

EXXON VALDEZ
The oil spill from the tanker *Exxon Valdez* off Alaska in 1989 was an environmental disaster. The tanker hit a reef and about 42 million litres (11 million gallons) of oil leaked out and spread along 1,900 km (1,180 miles) of coastline. Over 250,000 seabirds, 2,800 sea otters, 300 seals, and many other animals died. Experts think the area could take 30 years to recover. Money paid by ExxonMobil in compensation for the damage has been used to enlarge Alaska's Kenai Fjords National Park.

Refining oil

To TURN IT INTO USABLE FORMS, crude oil is processed at an oil refinery. Here, crude oil is separated into different components to produce petrol and hundreds of other products, from jet fuel to central heating oil. Refining involves a combination of "fractional distillation" and "cracking". Fractional distillation separates out the ingredients of oil into "fractions", such as light oil or heavy oil, using their different densities and boiling points. Cracking splits the fractions further into products such as petrol by using heat and pressure to "crack" heavy, long-chain hydrocarbon molecules into shorter, lighter ones.

OIL IN STORE

When crude oil arrives from the oil fields by pipeline or ship, it is stored in giant tanks ready for processing. Oil volume is usually measured in "barrels", with one barrel being equivalent to 159 litres (35 gallons). A typical large oil refinery can hold about 12 million barrels of crude oil in its tanks – enough to supply the whole of the USA with oil for about three-quarters of a day.

REFINERY COMPLEX

A typical refinery, like this one at Jubail in Saudi Arabia, is a gigantic complex of pipework and tanks covering an area the size of several hundred soccer fields. The pipe still is the large tower on the far left of the picture below. Big refineries operate around the clock, 365 days a year, employing some 1,000–2,000 people. The workers mostly regulate activities from inside control rooms. Outside, refineries are surprisingly quiet, with just the low hum of heavy machinery.

At 20°C (68°F) only four hydrocarbons remain. Methane and ethane are used to make chemicals. Propane and butane are bottled for portable gas stoves and lamps

Petrol condenses at 20–70°C (70–106°F). It is mostly used as fuel for cars

Naphtha, which condenses at 70–160°C (160–320°F), is made into plastics, chemicals, and motor fuel

Paraffin, which condenses at 160–250°C (320–480°F), can be used for jet fuel, heating, and lighting, and as a paint solvent

Gas oil condenses at 250–350°C (480–660°F). It is used to make diesel fuel and central heating oil

Mixture of crude oil gases at 400°C (750°F) passes into the pipe still

Gases rise up the tower via holes in the trays called bubble caps

SPLITTING BY FRACTIONS

Fractional distillation involves heating crude oil until it turns to vapour. The hot vapour is then fed into a pipe still – a tall tower divided at intervals by horizontal trays. The heaviest fractions cool quickly, condense to liquid, and settle at the bottom. Medium-weight fractions drift upwards and condense on trays midway up the tower. The lightest fractions, including petrol, rise right to the top before condensing.

The heaviest hydrocarbons condense as soon as they enter the column

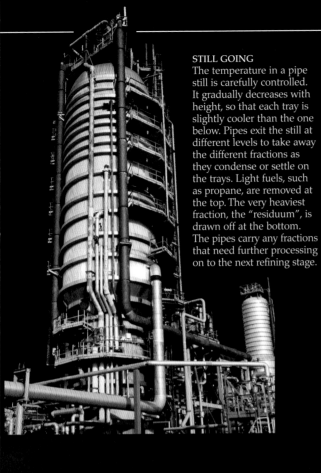

STILL GOING
The temperature in a pipe still is carefully controlled. It gradually decreases with height, so that each tray is slightly cooler than the one below. Pipes exit the still at different levels to take away the different fractions as they condense or settle on the trays. Light fuels, such as propane, are removed at the top. The very heaviest fraction, the "residuum", is drawn off at the bottom. The pipes carry any fractions that need further processing on to the next refining stage.

FLEXICOKER
Early refineries were able to use only a small proportion of crude oil. Just one quarter of each barrel, for example, could be turned into petrol. Today, over half is made into petrol, and most of the rest can be made into useful products, too. Flexicokers can convert previously wasted residuum into lighter products such as diesel. At the end of the process, an almost pure-carbon residue called coke is left, which is sold as solid fuel.

CRACKING TIME
Some fractions emerge from the pipe still ready for use. Others must be fed into bullet-shaped crackers like those above. While some petrol is produced by pipe stills, most is made in crackers from heavy fractions using a process known as "cat cracking". This relies on intense heat (about 538°C/1,000°F) and the presence of a powder called a catalyst (the cat). The catalyst accelerates the chemical reactions that split up the hydrocarbons.

Materials from oil

OIL IS NOT JUST A SOURCE OF ENERGY – it is also a remarkable raw material. Its rich mix of hydrocarbons can be processed to give useful substances known as petrochemicals. Processing usually alters the hydrocarbons so completely that it is hard to recognize the oil origins of petrochemical products. An amazing range of materials and objects can be made from petrochemicals, from plastics to perfumes and bed sheets. We use many oil products as synthetic alternatives to natural materials, including synthetic rubbers instead of natural rubber, and detergents instead of soap. But oil also gives us entirely new, unique materials such as nylon.

COMING CLEAN
Most detergents are based on petrochemicals. Water alone will not remove greasy dirt from surfaces, since it is repelled by oil and grease. Detergents work because they contain chemicals called surface active agents, or surfactants, which are attracted to both grease and water. They cling to dirt and loosen it, so that it can be removed during washing.

LIVING WITH PETROLEUM
To show just how many ways we use oil, this American family was asked to pose outside their home with all the things in their house that are made from oil-based materials. In fact, they had to almost empty their home, since there were remarkably few things that did not involve oil. In addition to countless plastic objects, there were drugs from the bathroom, cleaning materials from the kitchen, clothes made from synthetic fibres, cosmetics, glues, clothes dyes, footwear, and much more besides.

Oil in lipstick acts as a lubricant

Lipstick

LOOKING GOOD
Lipstick, eyeliner, mascara, moisturizer, and hair dye are just some of the many beauty products that are based on petrochemicals. For example, most skin lotions use petroleum jelly – a waxy, paraffin-like material made from oil – as a key ingredient. Some brands advertise their ranges as "petroleum-free" if, unusually, they do not contain oil products.

Eyeliner

Tough plastic moulded parts of car (polypropylene)

Clothes dyes

Clothes made from synthetic fibres

Cleaning fluids

House paint (acrylics)

Grass grown with the aid of fertilizers made from petrochemicals

DRESSING UP
Molecules in petrochemicals can be linked together to create a huge range of synthetic fibres, such as nylon, polyester, and Lycra®, each with its own special qualities. This microscopic picture shows how smooth acrylic fibre (red) is compared to sheep's wool (cream). Acrylic dries faster than wool, because its fibre strands have no rough edges for water drops to cling to.

Synthetic acrylic fibre

Natural wool fibre

FEELING BETTER
From the very earliest days, oil was known for its supposed medicinal qualities. In the Middle Ages, it was used for treating skin diseases. Now it is a source of some of our most important drugs, such as steroids and the painkiller aspirin, both of which are hydrocarbons.

Aspirin

Plastic moulding for radios, TVs, and computers (polystyrene)

Foam cushions (polyurethane)

Hard-wearing playthings (PVC and HDPE)

Plastic safety windows (PVC)

Food storage boxes (polythene)

Lightweight eyeglass lenses (polycarbonate)

Shatterproof containers (polycarbonate)

Hot-water bottle (synthetic rubber)

READING OIL
As you read this book and look at the pictures, you are looking at oil. This is because printing ink is made from tiny coloured particles (pigment) suspended in a special liquid called a solvent. The solvent is usually a paraffin-like liquid distilled from crude oil. Paints and nail varnishes also use petroleum-based solvents as pigment-carriers.

COLOURFUL CANDLE
Candles can be made from beeswax and other natural waxes, but most cheap candles are made from paraffin wax. To produce this odourless wax, oil is filtered through clay and treated with sulphuric acid. Colour can be added to make the candles more attractive. Paraffin wax is also used in polishes, crayons, and many other products.

Paraffin-wax candle

Plastics and polymers

PLASTICS PLAY an incredibly important part in the modern world. They find their way into our homes in many different ways and forms, from boxes used to keep food fresh to TV remote controls. Plastics are essentially materials that can be heated and moulded into almost any shape. They have this quality because they are made from incredibly long, chain-like molecules called polymers. Some plastic polymers are entirely natural, such as horn and amber. But nearly all the polymers we use today are artificially made, and the majority of them are produced from oil and natural gas. Scientists are able to use the hydrocarbons in oil to create an increasing variety of polymers – not only for plastics, but also to make synthetic fibres and other materials.

18th-century tortoiseshell snuff box

NATURAL POLYMERS
In the past, people made buttons, handles, combs, and boxes from natural polymers such as shellac (secretions of the lac insect) and tortoiseshell (mostly the shells of hawksbill turtles). A tortoiseshell box like this was made by heating and melting the tortoiseshell, and then letting it cool and solidify in a mould.

MAKING POLYMERS
Polymers are long-chain molecules made up of smaller molecules called monomers. Polythene (or polyethene), for example, is a plastic polymer made from 50,000 molecules of a simple hydrocarbon monomer called ethene. Scientists make the ethene monomers join together in a chemical reaction known as polymerization. Worldwide, over 60 million tonnes of polythene are produced each year.

Each ethene monomer in the chain has two hydrogen atoms (white) and two carbon atoms (black)

Polythene polymer

EARLY PLASTIC
The first semi-synthetic plastic, called Parkesine, was created by Alexander Parkes (1813–90) in 1861. It was made by modifying cellulose, the natural polymer found in cotton. The age of modern plastics began in 1907, when Leo Baekeland (1863–1944) discovered how to make new polymers using chemical reactions. His revolutionary polymer, called Bakelite, was made by reacting phenol and formaldehyde under heat and pressure. Bakelite had many uses, from aircraft propellers to jewellery and door knobs, but its greatest success was as a casing for electrical goods, since it was an excellent electrical insulator.

Bakelite telephone

COMMON PLASTICS
Hydrocarbons can be linked together in different ways to form hundreds of different types of plastic polymer, each with its own special qualities. When polymer strands are held rigidly together, for example, the plastic is stiff like polycarbonate. When the strands can slip easily over one another, the plastic is bendy like polythene. So the makers of plastic items can select a plastic that gives just the right qualities for the intended use.

POLYTHENE
Tough yet soft and flexible, polythene, or polyethene, is one of the most versatile and widely used of all plastics. First made by the ICI company in 1933, it is also one of the oldest plastics. Most plastic drinks bottles are made of polythene.

HDPE
There are many kinds of polythene, including HDPE (high density polyethene). HDPE is an especially tough, dense form of polythene that is often used to make toys, jugs, detergent bottles, and rubbish bins.

LDPE
In LDPE (low density polyethene), the polymers are only loosely packed, making a very light, very flexible plastic. Clear LDPE film is widely used for packaging bread and as a kitchen food-wrap.

PVC
PVC (polyvinyl chloride), one of the hardest plastics, is used for sewer pipes and window frames. When softened by substances called plasticizers, it can be used to make shoes, shampoo bottles, medical blood bags, and much more.

POLYPROPYLENE
A rugged plastic that resists most solvents and acids, polypropylene is often used for medicine and industrial chemical bottles. Photographic film is also made of polypropylene, as the plastic is not harmed by the chemicals used in the developing process.

FAST FIBRES
Not all hydrocarbon polymers are plastics. The polymers can also be strung together to make light, strong fibres. Synthetic polymer fibres are used not only use to make everyday clothes, but also to produce special items of sportswear. Based on studies of shark skin, this Fastskin® swimsuit is designed to let the swimmer glide through the water with the least resistance.

CARBON-POWER
By embedding fibres of carbon in them, plastics such as polyester can be turned into an incredibly strong, light material called carbon fibre reinforced plastic (CFRP or CRP). Because it combines plastic and carbon, CRP is described as a composite material. It is ideal for use where high strength and lightness need to be combined, as in the artificial limbs of this sprinter.

CRP is as tough as metal, but can be moulded into any shape

FOOTBALL BUBBLE
Plastic polymers do not have to be hydrocarbons made from oil or natural gas. In fluorocarbon polymers such as Teflon® (used to coat non-stick cooking pans) and ethylene tetrafluoroethylene (ETFE), it is not hydrogen but fluorine that links up with carbon. ETFE can be made into tough, semi-transparent sheets, like those shown here covering the futuristic Allianz Stadium in Munich. The stadium glows red when the Bayern Munich soccer team plays at home.

Aramid fibres

TOUGH THREADS
In 1961, DuPont™ chemist Stephanie Kwolek (b.1923) discovered how to spin solid fibres from liquid chemicals including hydrocarbons. The resulting fibres, called aramid fibres, are amazingly tough. Aramid fibres such as Kevlar® can be woven together to make a material that is light enough to wear as a jacket, yet tough enough to stop a bullet.

Kevlar® bullet-proof vest

POLYSTYRENE
When moulded hard and clear, polystyrene is used to make items such as CD cases. Filled with tiny gas bubbles, it forms the light foam used to package eggs. This foam is also used for disposable coffee cups, because it is a good heat insulator.

POLYCARBONATE
Being hard to break and capable of withstanding quite high temperatures, polycarbonate is becoming increasingly popular in manufacturing. DVDs, MP3 players, electric light covers, and sunglass lenses are all typically made with polycarbonate.

Big oil

Oıl has made individuals wealthy, brought huge profits to companies, and transformed poor countries into rich ones. Right from the early days of oil in the 19th century, oil barons made fortunes almost overnight. In Baku, there was Hadji Taghiyev (1823–1924). In America, the first oil millionaire was Jonathan Watson (1819–94) of Titusville, where Drake drilled the first US oil well (p.12). Then came the great oil dynasties of John D. Rockefeller (1839–1937) and Edward Harkness (1874–1940), and later the Texas oil millionaires such as Haroldson Hunt (1889–1974) and Jean Paul Getty (1892–1976) – each acclaimed at one time as the richest man in the world. In the late 20th century, it was Arab sheikhs who were famous for their oil wealth. Now it is Russia's turn.

THE FIRST OIL GIANT
Standard Oil began as a small oil refining company in Cleveland, Ohio, USA, but it quickly grew into the first giant oil company and made the fortunes of Rockefeller and Harkness. In the 1920s and 30s, the company became famous throughout the developed world as Esso, and Esso filling stations like this one in New Jersey became a familiar sight. Now called ExxonMobil, it is the biggest of the giant oil companies.

The Emirates Tower is one of the world's tallest buildings

OIL SHEIKH
The huge reserves of oil in the Middle East have made many Arab sheikhs immensely rich – none more so than Sheikh Zayed bin Sultan Al Nahyan. Sheikh Zayed (1918–2004) was one of the richest men of all time, worth £23 billion. Popular and generous, he became the first president of the United Arab Emirates (UAE).

OIL TOWERS
Oil wealth has transformed countries such as Saudi Arabia, UAE, and other states along the Persian Gulf. Half a century ago, these were largely poor countries where desert nomads lived simply, as they had done for thousands of years. The economies of these countries are now booming, and gleaming modern cities like Dubai City in the UAE are rising amid the sands.

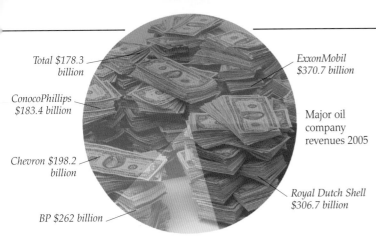

Total $178.3 billion

ConocoPhillips $183.4 billion

Chevron $198.2 billion

BP $262 billion

ExxonMobil $370.7 billion

Major oil company revenues 2005

Royal Dutch Shell $306.7 billion

Chelsea player, Michael Ballack

Roman Abramovich

BIG OIL, BIG MONEY
There are thousands of commercial oil companies, of all different sizes, including ExxonMobil, which became the world's largest company in 2005. In fact, the combined revenues of the six biggest commercial oil companies in 2005 was a staggering $1,499.3 billion, which is almost equal to the size of the entire Russian economy.

RUSSIAN RICHES
When the Soviet Union broke up in the 1990s, many state oil and gas companies were sold off cheaply. Astute Russian investors, such as Mikhail Khodorkovsky and Roman Abramovich, bought into them and became billionaires. Abramovich used his wealth to buy London's Chelsea soccer club, making him a celebrity and the club successful.

1959 Cadillac Eldorado convertible

GAS-GUZZLER
Seemingly endless supplies of cheap oil in the USA meant that everyone benefited from oil wealth and even ordinary people could afford to run big cars. Between the 1950s and 1970s, many Americans cruised the highways in gigantic, glamorous cars like this 1959 Cadillac. Nowadays, people are more fuel-conscious, and cars are generally smaller. Nonetheless, "gas-guzzlers" remain status symbols for the better-off.

Waste gas from oil production is burned off or flared

BP solar cells in the Philippines

In 2000 BP changed its logo to a flower symbol

OUTSIDE THE OIL BOOM
Governments do not always ensure that everyone benefits from the riches brought by oil. Since oil is often found in poor countries, the contrast between rich and poor is often very marked. While the city of Lagos in Nigeria booms, here in the Niger Delta, poor local Urohobo people bake *krokpo-garri* (tapioca) in the heat of a gas flare. Exposure to pollutants from oil and gas flares can cause serious health problems.

GOING GREEN
Pollution caused by oil spills and burning oil has given oil a bad name. In recent years, some oil companies have worked hard to present a cleaner, greener image, and begun investing in alternative energy. BP, for example, now has a large share of the solar power market. It has been part of the world's biggest ever solar energy scheme, which provides solar power for isolated villages in the Philippines.

The struggle for oil

OIL IS SO CENTRAL to the modern way of life that countries have gone to war over it. Oil is crucial to the prosperity of a nation, providing energy to fuel everything from its transport networks to its industries. It can also be vital to a nation's survival, since many of the military machines that protect it run on oil. So it is not surprising that oil was at the heart of many conflicts in the 20th century, and plays a key part today in many confrontations. The enormous oil reserves of Middle Eastern countries such as Iran and Iraq have kept them in the forefront of global news and guaranteed the world's continuing interest in their affairs. Now the exploitation of reserves in Russia, Venezuela, Nigeria, and other countries is making the politics of oil even more complex.

FUELLING THE NAVY
Oil giant BP began as the Anglo-Persian Oil Company, founded after oil was discovered in Iran in 1908. This was the first big oil company to use Middle Eastern oil. Its oil was vital to Britain in World War I (1914–18), as its oil-powered battleships won out over Germany's coal-powered ships.

MOSSY'S DOWNFALL
Mohammed Mossadegh (1882–1967) was the popular, democratically elected prime minister of Iran from 1951 to 1953. He was removed from power in a coup supported by the USA and Britain after he nationalized the assets of the British-controlled Anglo-Iranian (formerly Persian) Oil Company.

Sheikh Yamani was famed for his shrewd negotiating skills

OIL LEADER
In the 1960s, the key oil-producing nations, including those of the Middle East, formed OPEC (Organization of Petroleum Exporting Countries) to represent their interests. Saudi Arabia's Sheikh Yamani (b.1930) was a leading OPEC figure for 25 years. He is best known for his role in the 1973 oil crisis, when he persuaded OPEC to quadruple oil prices.

THE OIL CRISIS
In 1973, war broke out between Israel and Arab forces led by Syria and Egypt. OPEC halted all oil exports to Israel's supporters, including the USA and many European nations. This led to severe oil shortages in the West, which had long relied on Middle Eastern oil, and long queues for petrol. US filling stations sold fuel to drivers with odd- and even-numbered plates on alternate days.

Petrol can

THE FIRES OF WAR
Oil has played a key role in the wars that have rocked the Persian Gulf region over the last 20 years. When Iraqi dictator Saddam Hussein's troops invaded Kuwait in 1990, he claimed that Kuwait had been drilling into Iraqi oil fields. And when America and its allies intervened to liberate Kuwait, they were partly motivated by the need to secure oil supplies. The retreating Iraqis set light to Kuwaiti oil wells (right).

MILITARY PRESENCE
The US has several large military bases in the Middle East. One purpose is to keep planes and troops on hand to guard against any disruption to oil supplies which could wreak havoc on the world economy. While some Arab states like the sense of security brought by the American presence, these military bases remain a source of tension in the region.

F14 Tomcat

ARCH TERRORIST
Osama bin Laden's terrorist organization Al Qaeda has been behind many terrible attacks on innocent people in recent years. He claims that one of the motivations for these attacks is the West's – and especially America's – concern for Middle Eastern oil, and its military presence in the region to protect it.

Osama bin Laden

Orange was the campaign colour of the Our Ukraine party

ORANGE REVOLUTION
With vast oil and gas reserves, Russia is the world's new oil power. In future, Russia may use its energy muscle to try to exert control over its neighbours, as it did in 2006 when it steeply increased the price of gas supplies to Ukraine. Some people wonder if this might undermine the 2005 Orange Revolution (left), in which Ukrainians voted against Russian influence in their country's affairs.

The Kuwaiti oil fires started by Iraqi troops burned for seven months and consumed a billion barrels of oil

OIL FOR CHINA
China may soon overtake the USA as the world's biggest consumer of oil. The Chinese economy is expanding at an astonishing pace, with industry and construction booming and car-ownership rising steeply. China's own oil resources are insufficient to support this economic growth, so it must secure oil from overseas. In the process, it may change the balance of oil power dramatically.

Dirty oil

OIL BRINGS HUGE BENEFITS in energy and materials, but at a cost to the planet. Temperatures have always fluctuated naturally, but it now seems certain that burning fossil fuels is at the heart of the changes to the atmosphere that are making Earth warmer. The consequences of global warming could be devastating, bringing droughts, floods, and violent storms. Oil is not the only culprit, but few doubt that it is a major contributor. Oil spills can pollute rivers and seas, too, while fuel particles in the air may damage our health.

MESSAGE IN THE ICE
The evidence for global warming has been building up over recent years, and few scientists now doubt that it is happening. This scientist is examining an ice core (column of ice) taken from the ice cap in Greenland. Ice cores contain tiny air bubbles that became trapped when the water froze into ice. Ice cores from deep within the ice cap give a snapshot of the levels of greenhouse gases in the atmosphere when the ice formed thousands of years ago. It seems that greenhouse gases are now at a higher level than they have been for a very long time.

STORM WARNING
The greenhouse effect not only warms up the air, but also pumps it so full of energy that experts believe the weather could become much stormier as global temperatures rise. This is not to say that storms will happen all the time; it is simply that bad storms will become more frequent and more severe. Although it cannot be proved, some people argue that the bad season of hurricanes that hit the USA in 2005, culminating in Hurricane Katrina, was a symptom of global warming.

Solar radiation warms Earth

Sun

THE GREENHOUSE EFFECT
Solar radiation warms up the ground, which then re-emits infrared radiation back into the atmosphere. Much of this escapes into space, but some is trapped by certain gases in the atmosphere, such as carbon dioxide, water vapour, and methane, which act like the glass in a greenhouse. This "greenhouse effect" keeps Earth warm enough to sustain life. However, burning fossils fuels may have put so much extra carbon dioxide into the atmosphere that it is now perhaps trapping too much infrared radiation, making Earth warmer.

Greenhouse gases surrounding Earth

Some infrared radiation re-emitted by the ground escapes into space

Some infrared radiation is trapped by greenhouse gases, making Earth warmer

MELT DOW
If the air warms up, one of the fir consequences could be th melting of the polar ice cap This threatens wildlife such polar bears with the loss of the habitat, and it may threate humanity too. The complete meltir of the polar ice would raise sea leve several metres, flooding many of th world's major cities – including New Yo and London – and entirely drownir low-lying islands such as the Maldive Not everyone agrees with this worryir scenario, but there is now clear eviden that the ice caps are indeed meltir

DIRTY AIR
Oil consumption can pollute the air in various ways, besides releasing greenhouse gases. For example, when cars burn petrol they can emit unburned hydrocarbons into the air. These hydrocarbons react with sunlight to form a toxic fog in large cities such as Los Angeles. Petrochemical plants like the one above are another source of air pollution, emitting gases and particles into the air, besides clouds of steam, as they process the oil.

Asthma inhaler

SOOT HAZARD
In some vehicle engines, especially diesels, the fuel is only partially burned. Unburned compounds then cluster together to form tiny black particles of soot. When you breathe in, soot can get into your lungs, where it may cause bronchitis, asthma, and even cancer. Children are especially vulnerable to the harmful effects of soot, and soot could be behind the rise in the number of children with asthma.

CLEANING UP
Scientists are working on ways to deal with oil pollution. Here scientists are experimenting with special plant fibres that may be able to clean polluted water. The fibres have just been added to the dish of water on the left, which has been "polluted" by the blue oil compounds. In the dish on the right, the fibres have cleaned up all the blue oil compounds.

Fibres take up the oil compounds

Clean water

Blue oil compounds

THE BLACK FOREST
Some companies are looking for new oil sources in tropical rainforests, which are home to over half of the world's plant and animal species. This could have a major impact on these vulnerable habitats. Forest is lost as trees are cleared for oil wells, pipes, and roads. Such clearance encourages other development in the shape of towns, agriculture, and industry, which in turn leads to further destruction of the rainforest.

Saving oil

FOR MORE THAN A CENTURY, the world's oil consumption has risen non-stop. But in future we must almost certainly use less oil because we face a double crisis. First of all, few people now doubt that burning oil and other fossil fuels is making the world's climate warmer – and most experts are convinced that we face disaster if we do not find ways to use less oil soon. Secondly, the world could actually be running out of oil anyway. Many experts now talk about "peak oil", by which they mean that oil production has reached a peak, or will do soon, and must inevitably dwindle as oil becomes scarcer and more difficult to extract. Our dependence on oil can be partly reduced by switching to alternative forms of energy, but many people feel that it is also vital to find ways of using less oil.

30 billion barrels of oil produced in 2004

1,292 billion barrels of known reserves (of which perhaps three-quarters is hard to get a[t])

Aerodynamic shape reduces the energy needed to travel fast

OIL GOING DOWN

Opinions differ about just how much oil i[s] left. The US government predicts that o[il] production will go on rising until 203[0.] Some experts believe, however, that it wi[ll] peak in the next few years, or may eve[r] have peaked already. Production from th[e] world's three largest fields – Mexico'[s] Cantarell, Kuwait's Burgan, and Saud[i] Arabia's Ghawar – is now declining. S[o] maintaining current production level[s] depends on finding more big reserves, o[r] using sources such as tar sands, fro[m] which it is more difficult to extract oi[l.]

The human energy used to propel a bicycle is renewable and non-polluting

DO SOME LEG WORK

The most environmentally friendly way of travelling is to walk or cycle. Many towns and cities have dedicated cycle lanes and paths to make cycling less hazardous and more enjoyable. Almost half of all the people in the UK admit to using a car or getting a lift for short journeys that they could easily make on foot or by bicycle.

Most vegetables could be grown locally

Local produce is usually fresh, avoiding the need to use energy for refrigeration

TAKE THE TRAIN

Rather than travel in cars we could take trains, trams, and buses, which use three to five times less energy per person for every kilometre travelled than private cars. Nowhere is energy squandered in cars more than in the USA, where less than 5 per cent of people travel to work on public transport. Research has shown that if just 10 per cent of Americans used public transport regularly, the country's greenhouse gas emissions could be cut by over 25 per cent.

SHOP LOCALLY

The food in a typical supermarket trolley has travelled thousands of kilometres to get there. So rather than drive to the supermarket and buy food transported from far way, we can save oil by shopping locally, especially at farmers' markets, where food comes direct from nearby farms.

CUT ENERGY USE

We can save energy in the home by using less. Turning down the heating thermostat by just one degree saves a huge amount of energy. So does turning off unused lights, and switching off TVs and computers rather than keeping them on standby. Installing energy-saving fluorescent light bulbs (right) can save even more, since they consume up to 80 per cent less electricity than normal bulbs.

Energy-saving light bulbs use less energy and last longer by staying cool

Most packaging can be recycled

RECYCLE WASTE

It almost always takes less energy to make things from recycled materials than from raw materials. Using scrap aluminium to make new drinks cans, for example, uses 95 per cent less energy than making the cans from raw aluminium ore. Unusually, it takes more energy to recycle plastic. However, it still saves oil because plastics are mostly made from oil.

About 40 million plastic bottles are thrown away each day in the USA

Angle of windows minimizes heat loss in winter

Windows let huge amounts of heat escape

Only thick walls cut heat loss to a minimum

REDUCE HEAT LOSS

By recording how hot surfaces are, an infrared thermogram image can reveal heat loss from a building. The thermogram above shows that this old house loses most heat through the windows and roof (the white and yellow areas). This is why it is important to double-glaze windows and insulate roofs to block off the heat's escape routes. Many new buildings now incorporate energy-saving features. The construction, design, and unusual shape of London's City Hall (left) give it a cool exterior. It uses 75 per cent less energy than a conventional building of the same size.

Thermogram of City Hall, London, UK

Succulent plants, such as sedum, are ideal for green roofs, since they tolerate water shortages and need little soil

GREEN ROOFS

In future, more and more roofs could be "green" like this one, covered in living plants such as sedums and grasses – not just in the country, but in cities too. Chicago, USA, for example, now has more than 250 office blocks with green roofs, and every new public building is given a green roof. Green roofs not only look attractive, but they also provide tremendous insulation, keeping the heat out in summer and holding it in during winter. This means that less energy is used for central heating and air conditioning.

Oil substitutes

CONCERNS OVER THE WORLD'S dwindling oil supplies and the effect that burning oil is having on Earth's climate have encouraged people to look for different ways to power vehicles. Nearly all the major motor manufacturers are now developing so-called "green" cars that use alternatives to oil. A few of these cars are already on sale, but most are still at the experimental stage. These green cars work in four main ways. Some use alternative biofuels, such as ethanol and methanol. Others, called hybrids, cut oil consumption by combining a conventional engine with an electric motor, and there are even cars that are powered entirely by batteries. In some green cars, fuel cells produce electricity from hydrogen to drive electric motors.

FUEL FROM RUBBISH?
Everyday, huge amounts of rubbish are dumped in holes known as landfills. There bacteria break down materials such as food and paper, releasing a gas that is about 60 per cent methane. Scientists are trying to find ways to collect this methane and use it as a fuel.

FUELS FROM PLANTS
Biofuels made from plants are renewable fuels, because we can grow more plants to replace the ones we use. Biofuels can be made by converting the sugar and starch in crops such as maize (corn) and sugar cane into ethanol, or by converting soya-bean, rapeseed, flaxseed, and other plant oils into biodiesel. Methanol can be produced from wood and farm waste. However, we consume so much oil that for biofuel to make a real impact, vast swathes of extra land would have to be ploughed up to grow biofuel crops. And biofuels are only a little cleaner than conventional fuels.

Beans grow inside pods

Soya

Maize contains carbohydrates that can be turned into ethanol

Seeds contain high-energy oil

Flax

Maize

Rapeseed

WILDLIFE AT RISK
If extra land has to be ploughed up to grow biofuel crops, wildlife may be put at risk. Intensive farming already makes it difficult for ground-nesting birds, including skylarks (above), to find suitable nesting sites, and insecticide use means that they struggle to find enough insects to feed their chicks.

54

HYDROGEN FROM METHANOL

One of the problems with cars powered by hydrogen fuel cells is that few filling stations have so far been adapted to supply hydrogen. So until hydrogen filling stations are widespread, hydrogen-powered cars will have to make their own hydrogen by extracting it from other fuels. Daimler-Chrysler's Necar 5 uses methanol as its hydrogen source. This can be supplied by pumps at conventional filling stations.

Daimler-Chrysler experimental Necar 5

Inside the converter vegetable oil is thinned by mixing it with a substance called a lye

Fuel cell is topped up with methanol from a cartridge

METHANOL PHONE

A mobile phone battery must be recharged by the mains supply after a few hours of use. But scientists are developing tiny fuel cells that generate their own electricity to recharge the battery using methanol as a fuel. At present, most methanol is made from natural gas, as it is cheaper than making it from plant matter. So using methanol would not necessarily alter our reliance on fossil fuels.

Biodiesel is drawn off from base of converter

KITCHEN POWER

A car engine can be altered to run on vegetable oil. The oil is obtained by crushing plants (straight vegetable oil, or SVO), or it can be waste vegetable oil from cooking (WVO). But the catering industry does not produce sufficient WVO to have much of an effect on petrol consumption. And, as with biofuels, making SVO would require huge amounts of extra land to be given over to growing crops for fuel.

HOME REFINERY

Simple home units like this can convert vegetable oil into a diesel fuel called biodiesel, which burns slightly more cleanly than conventional diesel fuel. In warmer countries, biodiesel will run in ordinary diesel-engined vehicles. In cooler climates, it needs to be mixed in with conventional diesel.

WATER AND SUNLIGHT

All cars may one day be powered by hydrogen, either using fuel cells or, as in BMW's experimental H2R, a traditional internal combustion engine adapted to burn hydrogen instead of petrol. A hydrogen car would produce no harmful exhaust gases. Hydrogen for filling the cars could be produced by using solar power to split water into hydrogen and oxygen. So the cars would effectively run on water and sunlight – the most renewable of all resources.

BMW H2R

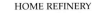

Wind power

FOR THOUSANDS OF YEARS, people have harnessed the power of the wind to drive sailing boats and turn windmills for grinding corn and pumping water. Today, wind power has been given a new boost thanks to wind turbines, which use the wind to generate electricity. The wind cannot be relied on to blow whenever we need electricity, but it is a clean and inexhaustible energy source – and, once the turbines have been built, inexpensive. Of all the forms of alternative energy, wind power is having the most impact. It still generates barely one per cent of the world's electricity, but it is making its mark in countries such as Denmark and Germany, where "wind farms" – groups of wind turbines – have sprung up in large numbers.

WIND PUMP
The famous "windmills" of the Netherlands were not actually mills but pumps for draining water from low-lying land. On North American farms, too, windmills were used to pump water – usually bringing up water from wells for cattle to drink. Instead of four big sails, North American wind pumps usually had a wheel with many small, angled blades, as shown here.

Paddle turns in the wind to ensure the bladed wheel faces directly into the wind

Stand could be mounted on a roof to catch the wind

Most wind turbines resemble aircraft propellers

WIND POWER AT HOME
In future, more and more houses are likely to have their own small, private wind turbine on the roof. Such generators might not supply all a home's energy needs, but they would reduce the energy needed from other sources. Domestic wind turbines are still expensive and quite noisy, but as designs improve they will almost certainly become quieter and cheaper.

OFFSHORE TURBINES
Because it is hard to find suitable sites on land with strong, reliable winds, turbines are sometimes built at sea. But erecting turbines at sea is difficult and expensive. The towers have to be taller, because they rest on the sea bed, and their foundations have to be laid underwater.

OLD WINDMILL
Windmills are thought to have originated in Persia in the 7th century CE, and reached their peak in the 18th century. The rotation of the sails turned two flat, round millstones, which ground corn between them. The sails were tilted so that they caught the prevailing wind at just the right angle. In post mills, the whole mill could turn around a central post to face into the wind.

Some mills had fabric sails like this; others had sails that resembled wooden shutters

SPINNING BLADES

In modern wind turbines, the turbine is mounted on top of a giant metal post that can be more than 90 m (295 ft) high. There are usually three blades, sometimes spanning over 100 m (330 ft), compared to the 60-m (200-ft) wingspan of a jumbo jet. Some people argue that wind turbines are good for the environment, because they provide clean energy. Others believe that they create eyesores when they are sited in parts of the country that are famed for their natural beauty. The spinning blades can also be hazardous for birds.

Gears increase the speed of rotation

Generator creates electricity

Nacelle

High-speed shaft

Tower supports assembly and carries electricity to ground

Turbine blade

ELECTRIC WIND

The workings of a wind turbine are in the long housing, or "nacelle", on top of the tower. As the wind drives the blades round, they spin a shaft that turns gears inside the nacelle. The gears increase the rotation speed enough to whirl magnets around inside a generator, which produces an electric current. Cables in the tower carry the current to the ground, where it is fed into the electricity supply grid. Automatic instruments on the nacelle alter the angle of the blades to suit the wind speed, and also turn the nacelle to face the wind.

WIND FARMS

Some wind turbines are erected singly or in pairs, but most are set up in clusters called wind farms. The largest offshore wind farms are off the coasts of Germany, the Netherlands, and the U.K. At present, most offshore wind farms have less than 80 turbines, but there are plans for building much larger assemblies. The largest onshore wind farms are in California, USA, where the Tehachapi farm has 4,600 turbines and can generate enough power to provide light for a city of half a million people.

BLOWING WITH THE WIND

The three-bladed rotor mounted on a steel tower is now the norm for wind turbines, but there are many other designs being tried out. One idea is to incorporate giant fans into the structure of new office buildings. Another is to mount turbines on gliders flying high enough to catch the powerful jet stream winds of the upper atmosphere. The Magenn company's airship-like design, shown here, is a turbine held aloft by a helium balloon. It too is designed to harness strong winds that blow far above the ground.

Surrounding the generator is a balloon of helium gas that holds it aloft

A tether holds the turbine in place and carries the electricity down to the ground

Solar energy

Nearly all of Earth's energy comes ultimately from sunlight, and so should be called solar energy. But when most people talk about solar energy they mean solar panels and collectors that harness the Sun's heat, and photovoltaic (PV) cells that convert sunlight into electricity. These devices can be used in a huge variety of ways, from providing the power for hand-held devices such as calculators to generating electricity for an entire city. Less than 0.5 per cent of the world's energy currently comes from solar power, but solar power's contribution is increasing rapidly as the price of PV cells comes down. One day, almost all homes may have arrays of PV cells on the roof, providing pollution-free energy all day long.

Dark absorber sheet soaks up Sun's warmth

Shiny reflector reflects warmth on to pipes

Water pipes made of copper conduct heat well

SOLAR HEAT
Solar panels use sunlight to provide heat. They are made of steel, glass, and plastic, and can heat either hot water or air. Inside each panel is a dark absorber sheet that warms up in the sunshine and heats pipes underneath carrying water or air. Over 1.5 million US homes now use rooftop panels like these, mostly to heat water for swimming pools.

SOLAR POWER STATION
Some solar power stations consist of large assemblies of solar collectors or PV arrays. This one in the Mojave Desert, California, USA, has hundreds of flat mirrors that direct sunlight at a central receiver mounted on a tower. In theory, a solar power station 260 sq km (100 sq miles) in area in a sunny place could generate all the electricity needed to supply the entire USA.

DISHES FOR THE SUN
Solar collectors reflect and concentrate the Sun's power. Typically either dish- or trough-shaped, their shiny surface collects sunlight from a wide area and focuses it on to a fluid-filled receiver. The sunlight heats the fluid, which in turn heats water for industrial processes or to create steam to turn turbines and generate electricity. Sophisticated collectors like these in Australia turn to track the Sun as it moves across the sky, so that they receive the maximum sunlight.

Dish tracks round with the Sun

Curved mirrors reflect sunlight on to the central receiver

The central receiver contains a fluid that is heated by sunlight

Solar cell

LIGHT CALCULATION

Many small electronic devices, including calculators and watches, have a PV cell or two to provide them with a permanent source of power. Each cell is a wafer of silicon material, rather like the chips in computers. When light strikes the cell, tiny electrically charged particles called electrons travel through the wafer to give a small electric current. It need not be sunlight – any reasonably bright light will do.

PV arrays are ideal for providing power in remote locations

Helios had a wing span of 75 m (247 ft)

Wing was covered by more than 60,000 PV cells, generating 35 kW of power

SOLAR POWER ON TAP

A single PV cell can generate barely enough power to light a small bulb, but it can be connected with others by wires to form a much larger assembly called an array. A PV array can provide enough electricity for a home or, as here, a lighthouse. More and more offices, public buildings, and factories are now being built with solar arrays on the roof to provide for their basic power needs.

FLYING BY SUNLIGHT

NASA's remote-controlled research aircraft *Helios* was just one of a number of experimental solar-powered cars and aeroplanes. As yet, they need too large an area of PV cells to provide enough power to make such machines a practical proposition. But if more efficient PV cells can be developed, cars and planes could one day be absolutely free to run, with zero exhaust emissions.

Hydrogen fuel cells powered Helios at night

SPACE POWER

The problem with solar power on the ground is that sunlight is weakened by the atmosphere and sometimes partially blocked by clouds, and it stops altogether at night. So NASA, the US space agency, is investigating the idea of giant sun-collecting disks 5 km (3 miles) across that could be attached to satellites orbiting Earth. Called power-beaming satellites, these would collect the streams of energy flowing from the Sun around the clock and beam it down to Earth as microwaves.

Water power

OF ALL THE FORMS OF RENEWABLE ENERGY, none is more established than water power. Today, water power provides a fifth of all the world's electricity. As with the wind, the power of running water was used by water wheels for thousands of years to grind corn and run simple machines. Now, however, water power is mostly used to generate electricity. Electricity generated in this way is called hydro-electric power, or HEP. The normal flow of most rivers is too weak to keep HEP generators turning. So usually a big dam must be built to "pond up" enough water to ensure a powerful flow. This means HEP is very expensive to set up, and it is hard to find suitable sites. Once running, though, HEP is very clean and very cheap.

OLD WATER WHEEL
Water wheels were the main source of industrial power in the days before engines and electricity. Water to turn the wheel was channelled either over the top of the wheel, as here (an overshot wheel), or underneath it (an undershot wheel). Gears and other mechanisms harnessed the motion of the wheel for driving millstones, pumps, timber saws, foundry hammers, weaving looms in textile factories, and much more besides.

Gate

Power lines carry electricity away from HEP station

Water flows from reservoir through gate into turbine

Generator rotor is turned by turbine, producing electricity

Water spins turbine

INSIDE A HEP STATION
A HEP station typically has a dam with electricity generators built into it. The water builds up behind the dam and falls with tremendous force when released. As gates in the dam open, water gushes down huge pipes and over the generator turbines. The pressure of the falling water spins the turbines, which in turn spin the generator rotors to produce electricity.

Water outflow has lost some energy

THE IMPORTANCE OF A BIG HEAD
In HEP, it is not simply the volume of water gushing over a dam that matters, but also the depth of the water behind the dam, or how far it falls. The deeper the water, or the farther it falls, the greater its pressure, or "head". The purpose of HEP dams is to build up a depth of water and a big head.

ASWAN PROS AND CONS
When the Aswan Dam was built across the Nile in Egypt in the 1960s, it supplied half of Egypt's electricity (now 15 per cent) and controlled the worst of the Nile's floods. But the lake it created drowned important archaeological sites, including the tomb of Abu Simbel, which had to be moved stone by stone to a new site. Furthermore, the Nile floodplain has become less fertile, because the nutrient-rich silt once deposited by the yearly floods is now held up behind the dam.

Tomb of Abu Simbel

Lake Mead extends for 180 km (110 miles) behind the Hoover Dam

The base of the Hoover Dam is over 200 m (660 ft) thick to withstand the huge pressure of water in the lake

HEP station

The town of Fengjie is demolished to make way for the Three Gorges Dam

HUGE DAMS
HEP dams are the largest artificial structures in the world. Completed in 1936, the Hoover Dam in the USA was for many years the world's tallest dam, at 221 m (726 ft) high. Behind it, in Lake Mead, it holds up the equivalent of two years of the Colorado River's water flow. When operating at full capacity, the Hoover Dam's HEP station can produce enough electricity to power a city of 750,000 people.

DROWNED VILLAGES
Sometimes dams are built in highly populated areas, requiring many people to be moved from their homes. The Three Gorges Dam project in China is thought to involve the relocation of about 1.2 million people. The dam itself, the world's largest, stretches 2.3 km (1.4 miles) from bank to bank. The lake behind it is 660 km (410 miles) long.

TIDAL POWER
Tides move huge volumes of water up and down river estuaries twice daily. To exploit this, a barrage can be built across the estuary and equipped with turbines that turn in both directions. These harness the flow of water when the tide is coming in and going out. But there are concerns that interfering with tidal flows could be harmful to the wildlife of estuary habitats. This tidal barrage at La Rance in France is one of few that has been built to date.

Nuclear power

Neutron

Energy released

Uranium nucleus splits, releasing more neutrons

Neutron

FISSION REACTION
Nuclear power works by splitting the nuclei of relatively large atoms, such as uranium or plutonium, to release energy This is called fission. The nuclei are split by firing tiny particles called neutrons at them. As the nuclei split they release more neutrons, which in turn split other nuclei, causing a chain reaction.

THE TINY NUCLEI (centres) of atoms contain huge amounts of energy. In a nuclear power station, nuclei are split apart to release this energy. A single 6-g ($^1/_3$-oz) pellet of nuclear fuel yields as much energy as a tonne of coal, and three of these pellets, weighing less than a teaspoon of sugar, could meet a family's energy needs for a year. At present, nuclear power stations provide 20 per cent of the world's electricity. While nuclear power produces no greenhouse gases, it is not problem-free. For example, it creates dangerous radioactive waste, and there is also a risk, however small, of an accident releasing floods of radiation or causing a nuclear explosion.

INSIDE A NUCLEAR POWER STATION
Like those that burn coal, oil, and gas, nuclear power stations create steam to drive turbines and generate electricity. But in this case, the heat to make the steam is made by splitting nuclei in a reactor. Inside the reactor's core, a fission chain reaction occurs in fuel rods made of uranium pellets. Special control rods absorb neutrons to slow the reaction so that heat is released gradually. A fluid called a coolant takes heat from the core to a steam generator.

Control rods adjust the rate of reaction

3. Heat from the core boils water in the steam generator

4. Steam turns turbines that drive electric generators

5. Generators produce electricity

Pylon carries high-voltage electricity

2. A pump circulates a coolant (yellow/orange) that carries heat from the core to the steam generator

Hot water goes to a cooling tower, where it loses its heat

Cold water returning from cooling tower

1. A fission chain reaction occurs in the fuel rods of the reactor's core

7. As the steam cools, it turns back into water and is pumped back to the steam generator

6. Pipes carrying cold water absorb the steam's heat

Reactor

NUCLEAR REACTOR
The heart of a nuclear power station is the reactor. There are various kinds of nuclear reactor. The first reactors, N-reactors, made plutonium for nuclear bombs. Most nuclear power stations have pressurized water reactors (PWRs), such as Spain's Vandellos-2 reactor shown here. PWRs use water as the fluid that cools the reactor, whereas advanced gas reactors (AGRs) are cooled by gas. A breeder is a type of reactor that actually creates more fuel than it "burns" as the fission reactions take place in the reactor's core.

Pylons

Control building

RADIOACTIVE WASTE

Nuclear power stations create radioactive waste that can cause cancer, mutations, and even sudden death. The deadly radioactivity eventually fades to nothing, but this may take 80,000 years. Most liquid waste is pumped out to sea, while gaseous waste is vented into the air. A stockpile of solid waste is building up as scientists decide what to do with it. Here, nuclear waste is being stored in water.

Nuclear warhead explosion

CHERNOBYL DISASTER

The worst nuclear accident happened on 25th April 1986 at the Chernobyl nuclear power station north of Kiev, in what is now Ukraine. A reactor overheated and burst its concrete containment building. Within days, dangerous radioactive dust had been spread by the wind across much of the globe, as this computer simulation shows. The area around Chernobyl is still uninhabitable, and thousands of local people have since died of cancers caused by exposure to radiation.

SPREADING WEAPONS

There is widespread concern that the spread of nuclear power will result in more countries developing nuclear weapons. This would increase the chances of a nuclear conflict – with potentially devastating consequences for the planet. Nuclear weapons work by either fission or fusion, and they are powerful enough to destroy whole cities.

Hydrogen nucleus with two neutrons

Hydrogen nucleus with one neutron

FUSION REACTION

When small hydrogen nuclei are smashed together, they fuse (join) together to form larger helium nuclei. Like fission, nuclear fusion releases energy. So far, fusion only works well in bombs. Researchers are trying to make it work in a more controlled way (cold fusion) to generate nuclear power without producing radioactive waste.

Nuclei collide and fuse

Helium nucleus forms

Energy given out

Neutron released

PLASMA TUBE

If cold fusion is successfully achieved, it will probably happen in a large circular tube called a torus, like the experimental one shown here. Inside the tube, hydrogen gas is heated until it forms a plasma (on the right of the picture) and begins to generate heat. Powerful magnetic fields contain the plasma within the tube.

Turbine and generator house

Production and consumption

THE WORLD IS NOW PRODUCING more oil than ever before. In 2006, the world's oil wells were pumping out nearly 85 million barrels of oil each day. Indeed, some experts believe that 2005 or 2006 may turn out to be the highest years of production of all time, and that such levels may never be reached again, because much of the most easily accessible oil is rapidly being used up. Oil consumption, too, has been rising for the last century, and there is no sign of any slow-down, despite worries about carbon dioxide emissions and global warming. It now looks as though, for the first time ever, oil consumption may start to exceed production, and so draw on stocks of oil already built up.

Saudi Arabia
10.37 million barrels per day

Saudi Arabia	264.3 billion barrels
Canada	178.8 billion
Iran	132.5 billion
Iraq	115 billion
Kuwait	101.5 billion
United Arab Emirates	97.8 billion
Venezuela	79.7 billion
Russia	60 billion
Libya	39.1 billion
Nigeria	35.9 billion

Offshore rigs extract oil from reserves deep under the sea bed

OIL RESERVES BY COUNTRY (2006)
The world's biggest subterranean oil reserves are in Saudi Arabia, whose Ghawar field is the world's largest oil field. Measuring over 280 km by 30 km (174 miles by 19 miles), the massive Ghawar field produces over 6 per cent of all the world's oil. Much of the rest of the world's oil is also underground in the Middle East. Canada has reserves that are almost as large as Saudi Arabia's, but most are in the form of oil sands, from which oil is difficult to extract.

= approximately 20 billion barrels

NEW OIL RESERVES
Estimates of oil reserves vary. According to some figures, the world's proven reserves have doubled in the last decade to well over 2,000 billion barrels, going up by 27 billion barrels per year. But this is mainly because previously uncounted reserves, such as Canada's oil sands, are now included. Only about 6 billion barrels of entirely new reserves are found each year. The largest undiscovered reserves may lie under the Arctic Ocean.

USA
20.5 million barrels per day

TOP CONSUMING NATIONS (2004)
The world consumes enough oil each year to fill a swimming pool 1.6 km (1 mile) square and 1.6 km (1 mile) deep. The USA is by far the most oil-thirsty nation in the world. Every day, it consumes well over 20 million barrels – a quarter of all the oil used in the world and more than three times as much as its nearest rival, China. Most of this oil goes into cars and trucks. China's consumption is going up as more Chinese take to the roads, but it is far behind America. India's consumption, too, is rising rapidly but it remains comparatively small. Consumption in most developed countries, including the UK, France, Germany, and Italy, hovers at around 2 million barrels a day, barely a tenth of that used by the USA.

Iran
4.09 million

Mexico
3.83 million

China
3.62 million

Norway
3.1 million

Canada
3.1 million

Venezuela
2.86 million

United Arab
Emirates
2.76 million

Russia
9.27 million

USA
8.69 million

TOP PRODUCING NATIONS (2004)

Just three countries – Saudi Arabia, Russia, and the USA – pump up over 40 per cent of the world's oil. More than 10 million barrels of oil a day are extracted from the reserves underneath Saudi Arabia, the world's single largest oil producer – enough to supply all of Western Europe with oil.

US OIL SOURCES (2005)

Although the USA is the world's third largest oil producer, it consumes so much that it actually has to import nearly 60 per cent of the oil it uses. Almost three quarters of the oil used in the USA comes from the Americas – from Canada, Mexico, Venezuela, and Colombia, as well as from the USA itself. Canada is the top source, exporting nearly 1.8 million barrels a day to its southern neighbour.
 The African countries of Nigeria, Angola, and Algeria supply around 12 per cent of the USA's oil needs, with the Middle East providing about the same amount again.

USA 42%

Canada 11%

Mexico 11%

Saudi Arabia 9%

Venezuela 8%

Nigeria 7%

Iraq 4%

25 other countries 8%

ExxonMobil (USA)
2,542 million barrels per day

Shell (UK/Netherlands)
1,959 million barrels

Chevron (USA)
1,931 million barrels

BP (UK)
1,507 million barrels

Yukos (Russia)
1,454 million barrels

DAILY PRODUCTION BY OIL COMPANIES (2003)

Although the "big six" American and European global oil corporations (p.47) earn the most money from oil, they are not all among the biggest producers. The Russian state-owned giant Yukos produces only a little less than BP. Indeed, when it comes to how much oil they have in the ground, the state-owned companies in Saudi Arabia, Iran, Russia, and Venezuela dwarf them.

China
6.5 million

Japan
5.4 million

Germany
and Russia
each with
2.6 million

Canada and
India each
with
2.3 million

Brazil
2.2 million

Timeline

FOR THOUSANDS OF YEARS, especially in the Middle East, oil was used for a variety of purposes, from burning in lamps to waterproofing roofs and making ships leakproof. However, the global oil age only really began about 150 years ago. The turning points were the introduction of the first paraffin lamps in 1857 and, more importantly, the invention of the internal combustion engine in 1862, which led to the development of the motor car. Today, oil not only dominates the world economy, but it is also a major influence in world politics.

Zoroastrian fire temple in Azerbaijan

C.4500 BCE
People in what is now Iraq use bitumen from natural oil seeps to waterproof their houses.

C.4000 BCE
People in the Middle East use bitumen to seal boats against leaks. This is called caulking, and it continues until the 1900s.

C.600 BCE
King Nebuchadnezzar uses bricks containing bitumen to build the Hanging Gardens of Babylon, and bitumen-lined pipes to supply the gardens with water.

Egyptian mummy case

500s BCE
Persian archers put bitumen on their arrows to turn them into flaming missiles.

450 BCE
The Ancient Greek historian Herodotus describes bitumen pits near Babylon, which are highly valued by the Babylonians.

C.300 BCE
Followers of the Zoroastrian religion build fire temples in places such as Azerbaijan. Natural gas from underground is used to fuel a constantly burning flame within the temple.

C.200 BCE
The Ancient Egyptians sometimes use bitumen when mummifying their dead.

C.1 BCE
The Chinese extract oil and gas when drilling for salt. They burn the gas to dry out the salt.

CE 67
Jews defending the city of Jotapata use boiling oil against Roman attackers.

100
The Roman historian Plutarch describes oil bubbling up from the ground near Kirkuk (in present day Iraq). This is one of the first historical records of liquid oil.

500s
Byzantine ships use "Greek fire" bombs made with bitumen, sulphur, and quicklime.

1264
The Venetian merchant and adventurer Marco Polo records seeing oil from seeps near Baku (in present day Azerbaijan) being collected in large quantities for use in medicine and lighting.

1500s
In Krosno, Poland, oil from seeps in the Carpathian Mountains is burned in street lamps.

1780s
Swiss physicist Aimé Argand's whale-oil lamp supersedes all other types of lamp.

C.1800
Tarmacadam (a mixture of graded gravel and tar) is first used to provide a good road surface.

1807
Coal gas provides the fuel for the world's first proper street lights in London, England.

1816
Start of the US coal gas industry in Baltimore.

1821
Natural gas is first supplied commercially in Fredonia, New York, USA, with gas being piped through hollow logs to houses.

1846
Canadian Abraham Gesner makes paraffin (kerosene) from coal.

1847
The world's first oil well is drilled at Baku, Azerbaijan.

1849
Abraham Gesner discovers how to make paraffin from crude oil.

1851
In Canada, Charles Nelson Tripp and others form North America's first oil company, the International Mining and Manufacturing Company, to extract asphalt from tar beds in Ontario.

1851
Scottish chemist James Young opens the world's first oil refinery at Bathgate, near Edinburgh, to produce oil from the rock torbanite, a type of oil shale.

1853
Polish chemist Ignacy Lukasiewiz discovers how to make paraffin from crude oil on an industrial scale. This paves the way for the paraffin lamp, which will revolutionize home lighting later in the decade.

Paraffin lamp

1856
Ignacy Lukasiewiz sets up the world's first crude oil refinery at Ulaszowice in Poland.

1857
American Michael Dietz patents a clean-burning lamp designed to burn paraffin, rather than the more expensive whale oil. within a few years, paraffin lamps will force whale-oil lamps off the market.

1858
North America's first oil well opens at Oil Springs, Ontario, in Canada.

1859
The USA's first oil well is drilled by Edwin L. Drake at Titusville, Pennsylvania.

1860
The Canadian Oil Company becomes the world's first integrated oil company, controlling production, refining, and marketing.

1861
Oil carried aboard the sailing ship *Elizabeth Watts* from Pennsylvania to London is the first recorded shipping of oil.

1862
Frenchman Alphonse Beau de Rochas patents the four-stroke internal combustion engine. Fuelled by petrol, it will power most cars in the 20th century.

1863
American businessman J. D. Rockefeller starts an oil refining company in Cleveland, Ohio.

1870
J. D. Rockefeller forms Standard Oil (Ohio), later known as Esso, and today as ExxonMobil.

1872
J. D. Rockefeller takes over 25 per cent of the US petroleum market. By 1877 he will control about 90 per cent of all oil refining in the USA.

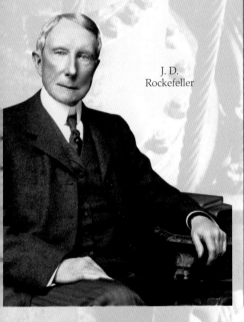

J. D. Rockefeller

Ford Model T

1878
The first oil well in Venezuela is set up at Lake Maracaibo.

1879
American Thomas Edison invents the electric light bulb.

1885
In Germany, engineer and industrialist Gottlieb Daimler invents the first modern-style petrol engine, using an upright cylinder and a carburettor to feed in the petrol.

1885
German engineer Karl Benz creates the world's first practical petrol-engined motor car for general sale.

1885
Oil is discovered in Sumatra by the Royal Dutch oil company.

1891
The Daimler Motor Company begins producing petrol engines in the USA for tram cars, carriages, quadricycles, fire engines, and boats.

1901
America's first deep oil well and gusher at Spindletop, Texas, trigger the Texas oil boom.

1905
The Baku oil field is set on fire during unrest throughout the Russian Empire against the rule of Tsar Nicholas II.

1907
The British oil company Shell and Royal Dutch merge to form Royal Dutch Shell.

1908
The first mass-produced car, the Model T Ford, is launched. As mass-production makes cars affordable to ordinary people, car ownership rises rapidly and demand for petroleum soars.

1908
Oil is found in Persia (modern Iran), leading to the formation of the Anglo-Persian Oil company – the forerunner of the modern oil giant BP – in 1909.

1910
The first oil discovery in Mexico is made at Tampico on the Gulf Coast.

1914–18
During World War I, British control of the Persian oil supply for ships and planes is a crucial factor in the defeat of Germany.

1932
Oil is discovered in Bahrain.

1935
Nylon is invented, one of the first synthetic fabrics made from oil products.

1935
Cat cracking is first used in oil refining. This uses intense heat and a substance called a catalyst to split up heavy hydrocarbons.

1938
Major oil reserves are discovered in Kuwait and Saudi Arabia.

Nylon rope

1939–45
World War II: the control of oil supplies, especially from Baku and the Middle East, plays a key role in the Allied victory.

1948
The world's largest liquid oil field is discovered in Ghawar, Saudi Arabia, holding about 80 billion barrels.

1951
The Anglo Persian (now Iranian) Oil Company is nationalized by the Iranian government, leading to a coup backed by the USA and Britain to restore the power of the Shah (king).

Timeline continues on page 68

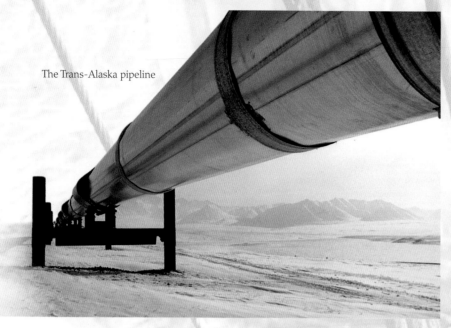
The Trans-Alaska pipeline

1960
OPEC (Organization of Petroleum Exporting Countries) is founded by Saudi Arabia, Venezuela, Kuwait, Iraq, and Iran.

1967
Commercial production of oil begins at the Alberta tar sands in Canada, the world's largest oil resource.

1968
Oil is found at Prudhoe Bay, northern Alaska. This becomes North America's major source of oil.

1969
In the USA, a vast oil spill started by a blow-out at a rig off the coast of Santa Barbara, California, does untold damage to marine life.

1969
Oil and natural gas are discovered in the North Sea, leading to a 25-year energy bonus for countries such as the UK.

1971
OPEC countries in the Middle East begin to nationalize their oil assets to regain control over their reserves.

1973
OPEC quadruples oil prices. It halts supplies to Western countries supporting Israel in its war against Arab forces led by Egypt and Syria. This causes severe oil shortages in the West.

1975
Oil production begins at North Sea oil rigs.

1975
In response to the 1973 oil crisis, the Strategic Petroleum Reserve (SPR) is set up in the USA to build up an emergency supply of oil in salt domes. By 2005, the USA will have 658 million barrels of oil stored in this way.

1977
The Trans-Alaska oil pipeline is completed.

1978
The tanker *Amoco Cadiz* runs aground off the French Coast, leading to a massive oil spill.

1979
A blow-out at the drilling rig Ixtoc 1 in the Gulf of Mexico results in the world's largest single oil spill.

1979–81
Oil prices rise from US $13.00 to $34.00 per barrel.

1989
The tanker *Exxon Valdez* runs aground in Prince William Sound, Alaska, causing an environmental catastrophe as oil spills on to the Alaskan coast.

Cleaning up after the *Exxon Valdez* oil spill

1991
Kuwaiti oilfields are set alight in the Gulf War.

1995
A UN resolution allows a partial resumption of Iraqi oil exports in the "oil for food" deal.

1996
Qatar opens the world's first major liquid natural gas (LNG) exporting facility.

2002
Construction on the BTU pipeline from Baku to the Mediterranean begins.

2003
The US Senate rejects a proposal to allow oil exploration in the Arctic National Wildlife Refuge (ANWR) in northern Alaska.

2003
A sour gas blow-out in Chongqing, southwest China, kills 234 people.

2004
US oil imports hit a record 11.3 million million barrels per day.

2004
North Sea production of oil and gas declines.

2005
Hurricane Katrina strikes the Gulf Coast, causing chaos in the US oil industry.

2005
The price of oil reaches US $70.80 per barrel.

2006
Russia stops gas supplies to Ukraine until the Ukranians agree to pay huge price rises.

2006
BP partially shuts down the Prudhoe Bay oil field due to corrosion of its Alaskan pipeline.

2007
In a dispute between Russia and Belarus over oil and gas supplies, Russia shuts down the transcontinental pipeline through Belarus, halting the flow of oil to countries in Western Europe.

A flooded oil installation in the USA hit by Hurricane Katrina in 2005

Find out more

THIS BOOK HAS GIVEN a taster of the world's largest and most complex industry, but your voyage of discovery need not end here. You can find out more about the geology of oil by exploring the rocks in your area and learning to identify the sedimentary rocks in which oil forms. You can also find out about the history, science, and technology of oil by visiting museums. Alternative energy centres and websites can tell you more about the environmental impact of oil consumption, and what we can do to reduce it.

USEFUL WEBSITES

- A list of specialist oil and gas museums around the world:
www.spe.org/spe/jsp/basic/0,,1104_1008232,00.html
- Virtual tour of the Fawley oil refinery, UK:
http://resources.schoolscience.co.uk/Exxonmobil/index.html
- Virtual tour of the Captain oil rig in the North Sea:
http://resources.schoolscience.co.uk/SPE/index.html
- A child's visit to an offshore oil rig:
www.mms.gov/mmskids/explore/explore.htm
- An in-depth look at the workings of an oil refinery:
http://www.citgo.com/CommunityInvolvement/Classroom/VirtualTours.jsp
- Students' page from the Society of Exploration Geophysics:
http://students.seg.org/K12/kids.htm
- Facts, games, and activities about energy, plus links:
www.eia.doe.gov/kids/index.html
- A US Department of Energy site about fossil fuels, including coal, oil, and natural gas:
www.fe.doe.gov/education/energylessons/index.html
- A comprehensive guide to oil refining:
http://science.howstuffworks.com/oil-refining.htm
- The Chevron company's Learning Centre, packed with facts:
www.chevron.com/products/learning_center/
- Basic geology, how oil forms, and how it is found:
www.priweb.org/ed/pgws/index.html
- All about fuel cells, from the Smithsonian Institute:
http://americanhistory.si.edu/fuelcells/
- An introduction to nuclear power from the USA's Nuclear Energy Institute:
www.nei.org/scienceclub/index.html
- The Alliance to Save Energy's kids site:
www.ase.org/section/_audience/consumers/kids
- Plenty of links on the topic "Recycle, Reduce, Reuse":
http://42explore.com/recycle.htm
- The USA's National Institute of Environmental Health Sciences site on recycling and reducing waste:
www.niehs.nih.gov/kids/recycle.htm

MUSEUM TRIPS

Many science and natural history museums have excellent exhibits covering topics raised in this book, including energy resources, fossil fuel formation, transport, and so on. If you are lucky, you may live near a specialist museum, such as the USA's Drake Well Museum in Titusville, Pennsylvania, and the California Oil Museum in Santa Paula, or the UK's National Gas Museum in Leicester.

Recycling can reduce our energy consumption

Waste materials for recycling

Museum model of an offshore rig

Panoramas and detailed views help to explain the refining process

Virtual tour of an oil refinery

VISITS AND VIRTUAL TOURS

Your school may be able to arrange a visit to an oil refinery or terminal, or to a filling station. The education departments of major oil companies can usually advise where this is possible. But oil installations are often sited in remote locations, and the processes that take place there may be too dangerous to make school visits possible, so virtual tours may be a better option. The Institute of Petroleum and ExxonMobil have set up virtual tours of the UK's Fawley oil refinery and the Captain oil rig in the North Sea. See the links in the Useful Websites box above.

Glossary

AEROGEL The lightest, lowest-density solid known. It is created artificially from silica and a liquid solvent such as ethanol.

ALKANES Hydrocarbons that have chain-like molecules.

ALTERNATIVE ENERGY Energy that does not come from fossil fuels. It includes solar, wind, water, and nuclear power.

ANTHRACITE The highest, most carbon-rich grade of coal, found deep underground.

Anthracite

ANTICLINE An area where the rock strata (layers) have been folded up into an arch.

AROMATICS Hydrocarbons with molecules containing one or more rings of carbon atoms.

ASPHALT A sticky, virtually solid form of oil, or an oil-based road surface. It is sometimes also called pitch, especially in processed form.

BENZENE A colourless liquid obtained from petroleum and used as fuel and in dyes. It is an aromatic hydrocarbon.

BIOFUEL Fuel made from organic material, typically plant oils, bacteria, and organic waste.

BIOGAS A gas produced when organic waste rots.

BITUMEN A treacly, semi-liquid form of oil, sometimes called tar, especially when in processed form.

BLOW-OUT An uncontrolled release from an oil well of oil and gas under pressure.

BORE The drill hole of an oil well.

BUTANE A flammable gas found in natural gas and used as a fuel for stoves.

CARBOHYDRATE A compound of carbon, hydrogen, and oxygen. Carbohydrate foods are key energy sources for plants and animals.

CARBON DIOXIDE A gas made by animals as they breathe out and used by plants for photosynthesis. It is also produced when fossil fuels are burned. Carbon dioxide is thought to be the main greenhouse gas responsible for global warming.

CARBONIFEROUS ERA The geological period 365–290 million years ago.

CAT CRACKING Using heat and a catalyst to break down heavy components of crude oil.

CATALYST A substance that speeds up chemical reactions.

COAL GAS A gas comprising mainly methane and hydrogen, made by distilling coal.

COAL TAR Tar made by refining coal.

CONDENSATE Liquid created when a vapour condenses. With petroleum, it refers to the thinner, more volatile portion of the oil.

CRUDE OIL Unprocessed petroleum in the form of a dark, sticky liquid.

DERRICK The tower that supports the drilling equipment in an oil well.

DRILL BIT An assembly of toothed wheels at the end of a drill string that cuts into the rock.

DRILL STRING The linked lengths of an oil well's drill, which are assembled piece by piece as the drill penetrates deeper into the ground.

DRILLING MUD A liquid-and-powder mix that is pumped around an oil drill. Drilling mud reduces friction, cools the drill bit, removes rock cuttings, reduces the risk of a blow-out, and helps to prevent the bore caving in.

ETHANE A flammable gas used as a fuel and as a coolant in refrigerators and air-conditioning units. It is found in petroleum and natural gas.

FAULT A crack in Earth's crust, where two giant slabs of rock slide past each other.

FLARING Burning off waste gas at an oil-well head.

Model of a benzene molecule

FORAMINIFERA Tiny sea creatures whose remains are believed to be a prime source material for oil.

FOSSIL FUEL A fuel made from plants and animals that lived long ago – essentially oil, natural gas, coal, and peat.

FRACTIONAL DISTILLATION The separation of different components in a liquid such as crude oil by heating it until it vaporizes, and then collecting the components as they condense at different temperatures.

FUEL CELL A battery that is kept continually charged by an input of fuel such as hydrogen.

GEOPHYSICAL SURVEY A method of mapping geological features using physical properties such as magnetism, gravity, and the reflection of seismic waves.

GLOBAL WARMING The gradual warming of Earth's climate, widely thought to be caused by a build-up of greenhouse gases in the atmosphere as a result of burning fossil fuels.

GREENHOUSE EFFECT The way that certain gases in Earth's atmosphere trap the Sun's energy, like the panes of glass in a greenhouse.

GREENHOUSE GAS One of several gases in the atmosphere that create the greenhouse effect, such as water vapour, carbon dioxide, and methane.

GUSHER A fountain of oil that erupts when a drill penetrates an oil pocket deep underground.

HYBRID CAR A car that uses both a petrol engine and an electric motor.

HYDRO-ELECTRIC POWER (HEP) Electricity generated by turbines that are driven by water pressure.

HYDROCARBON A chemical compound essentially containing hydrogen and carbon.

IMPERMEABLE Describing a material through which fluids (liquids and gases) cannot pass.

INSULATION The process of blocking the escape of heat or electricity, or a material that blocks the escape of heat or electricity.

INTERNAL COMBUSTION ENGINE An engine that gets its power by burning fuel inside cylinders.

KEROGEN The organic component of rock, formed by the breakdown of the trapped remains of plants and animals. Heat and pressure underground can "cook" kerogen and turn it into oil.

LIGNITE (BROWN COAL) The grade of coal with the least carbon, mined near the surface.

LIQUID NATURAL GAS (LNG) Natural gas turned into liquid form by cooling it to −160°C (−260°F).

METHANE A flammable gas, used as a fuel. It is the main ingredient in natural gas and animal flatulence. It is also a greenhouse gas.

NAPHTHENES Heavy-ring hydrocarbons.

NATURAL GAS Gas formed underground from the remains of long-dead sea life as part of the same process that produces crude oil.

NODDING DONKEY An oil-well pump with a beam that swings up and down with a motion that resembles a donkey nodding.

Nodding donkey

Refinery at night

NUCLEAR POWER Energy obtained by splitting the tiny nuclei (centres) of atoms inside a device called a nuclear reactor.

OCTANE An alkane hydrocarbon consisting of a chain of eight groups of hydrogen and carbon atoms.

OIL RIG A drilling platform.

OIL SANDS Deposits of sand and clay in which each grain is coated with bitumen.

OIL SHALE Rock, such as marlstone or shale, that is rich in kerogen.

OIL TRAP A place where oil builds up under a layer of trap rock.

OPEC The Organization of Petroleum Exporting Countries, which includes Algeria, Indonesia, Iran, Iraq, Kuwait, Libya, Nigeria, Qatar, Saudi Arabia, the United Arab Emirates, and Venezuela.

OPEN CAST A mine in which a mineral resource such as coal is extracted from near the surface by digging an open pit.

ORGANIC Related to, or derived from, plants or animals.

PARAFFIN A flammable liquid produced by distilling crude oil. It is used in lamps and as jet fuel. In the USA, paraffin is called kerosene.

PEAK OIL The idea that oil production will reach a peak soon, or may already have done so, and then dwindle as viable reserves run dry.

PEAT A soil-like organic material that forms in bogs. Peat contains enough carbon to be used as a fuel when it is dried out.

PERMEABLE Describing a material through which fluids (liquids and gases) can pass.

PETROCHEMICAL A useful substance produced by refining crude oil.

PETROL A fuel derived from crude oil, widely used in cars. Petrol is called gasoline in the USA.

PETROLEUM An energy-rich substance formed from fossilized organisms. Typically liquid, it may also be solid or gaseous.

PHOTOSYNTHESIS The process by which plants use sunlight to make carbohydrate food from water and gases in the air.

PHOTOVOLTAIC (PV) CELL A device that makes electricity from sunlight.

PHYTOLANKTON Tiny floating marine organisms that make their own food by photosynthesis. The remains of phytoplankton are thought to be one of the key source materials from which oil is formed.

PIG A device that separates batches of oil in a pipe or checks the pipe for defects.

PITCH A thick, toffee-like black substance made either naturally as part of crude oil, or synthetically by processing oil or coal. Natural pitch is more properly known as asphalt.

PLASTIC A material that can be heated and moulded into almost any shape. Most plastics are made from hydrocarbons extracted from oil.

POLYMER An incredibly long, chain-like molecule, or a material made from such molecules. Plastics are polymers.

POROUS Describing a material, such as rock, that is full of tiny holes (pores), like a sponge.

PROPANE A flammable gas extracted from natural gas, used as a fuel and in refrigeration.

REFINERY An industrial site where crude oil is processed (refined) into usable products.

RENEWABLE ENERGY Energy from sources that are continually replenished, including wind, solar, and water power, and biofuels. Fossil fuels, such as oil, are non-renewable energy sources, since we cannot replace the fuel we use.

RESERVOIR ROCK Rock containing pores and cracks in which oil accumulates.

RESIDUUM The thick, heavy part of crude oil left behind after fractional distillation.

SALT DOME An underground salt deposit.

SEAM A layer of a mineral such as coal.

SEDIMENTS Deposits of sand and grit laid down by water or wind.

SEEPS Places where crude oil oozes naturally up to the surface.

SOLAR POWER Energy produced from devices called solar panels and solar collectors, which absorb or focus sunlight to heat fluids, or from photovoltaic (PV) cells.

SOURCE ROCK Rock in which oil forms and then migrates to reservoir rock.

TAR A thick, treacly substance formed naturally from crude oil or by processing crude oil or coal. Natural tar is usually called bitumen.

TRAP (CAP) ROCK A layer of impermeable rock such as shale that traps oil to form deposits.

TURBINE A set of blades that rotates when struck by a moving fluid.

VISCOSITY How resistant a liquid is to flowing, or how thick and sticky it is.

VOLATILE Describing a liquid that evaporates easily at low temperatures.

WELL-LOGGING The process of analysing the rocks in an oil bore (drill hole).

WILDCAT WELL An exploration well drilled outside any known region of oil production.

WIND FARM A group of wind turbines.

WIND TURBINE A device that uses the wind to generate electricity.

Wind farm

Index

AB

Acknowledgements

The publisher would like to thank: Hilary Bird for the index; Dawn Bates for proofreading; Claire Bowers, David Ekholm-JAlbum, Clarie Ellerton, Sunita Gahir, Marie Greenwood, Joanne Little, Susan St Louis, Steve Setford, and Bulent Yusef for help with the clipart; David Ball, Kathy Fahey, Neville Graham, Rose Horridge, Joanne Little, and Sue Nicholson for the wallchart.

The publishers would also like to thank the following for their kind permission to reproduce their photographs:

(Key: a-above; b-below/bottom; c-centre; f-far; l-left; r-right; t-top)

The Advertising Archives: 15tr, 15bc; akg-images: 12cl; Alamy Images: AGStockUSA, Inc. 39tc; Bryan & Cherry Alexander Photography 20–21b, 35b; allOver Photography 53br; Roger Bamber 37cra; G.P. Bowater 34tl, 39tr; Nick Cobbing 50tl; Richard Cooke 52l; John Crall / Transtock Inc. 15l; CuboImages srl 21cr; Patrick Eden 60–61c; Paul Felix Photography 23br; The Flight Collection 49tr; David R. Frazier Photolibrary, Inc. 54tl; Paul Glendell 56ftr; Robert Harding Picture Library Ltd 51t; imagebroker / Stefan Obermeier 45br; ImageState 50ca; André Jenny 52br; kolvenbach 41cl; Lebrecht Music and Arts Photo Library 11bl; Kari Marttila 45fcl; Gunter Marx 70br; North Wind Picture Archive 11br; Phototake Inc. 19cra; Popperfoto 9c; Patrick Steel 48bc; Stock Connection Blue 36–37c; Angel Svo 21tc; Visual Arts Library (London) 8b; mark wagner aviation-images 41b; Worldspec / NASA 7tr; Courtesy of Apple. Apple and the Apple logo are trademarks of Apple Computer Inc., registered in the US and other countries: 6c, 69br (Laptop); The Art Archive: 8tr; Bibliothèque des Arts Décoratifs Paris / Dagli Orti 61cra;

Biodys Engineering: 55tr; Courtesy of BMW: 55b; Provided by BP p.l.c.: 47crb, 47br, 64–65 (Background), 66–67 (Background), 68tl, 68–69 (Background), 69br (On Screen), 70–71 (Background); The Bridgeman Art Library: Private Collection, Archives Charmet 9tl; Corbis: 27tr; Bettmann 12tc, 12tr, 14c, 48c, 67bl; Jamil Bittar / Reuters 51bl; Lloyd Cluff 35tr; Corbis Sygma 49cra; Eye Ubiquitous / Mike Southern 59tr; Natalie Fobes 68c; Lowell Georgia 31tr; Martin Harvey / Gallo Images 37bc; Hulton-Deutch Collection 21tl; Hulton-Deutsch Collection 14bl, 15c; Langevin Jacques / Corbis Sygma 35cra; Ed Kashi 47bl; Karen Kasmauski 37br; Matthias Kulka 65t; Lake County Museum 40tl; Jacques Langevin / Corbis Sygma 46c; Lester Lefkowitz 6–7bc; Stephanie Maze 33cl; Francesc Muntada 62–63b; Kazuyoshi Nomachi 39b; Stefanie Pilick / dpa 23t; Jose Fuste Raga 46b; Roger Ressmeyer 38tl, 40cl, 63tl; Reuters 32tc; Otto Rogge 58br; Bob Rowan / Progressive Image 29c; Grafton Marshall Smith 58cr; Lara Solt / Dallas Morning News 26tl; Paul A. Souders 61tr; Stocktrek 63tr; Ted Streshinsky 35tl; Derek Trask 6bl; Peter Turnley 48–49c; Underwood & Underwood 13br; Tim Wright 29t; DaimlerChrysler AG: 55tc; DK Images: The British Museum 9cl, 66bl; Simon Clay / Courtesy of the National Motor Museum, Beaulieu 14tl; Tim Draper / Rough Guides 19tl; Neil Fletcher / Oxford University Museum of Natural History 2bl, 23bl; Peter Hayman / The British Museum 9tr; Chas Howson / The British Museum 9crb; Jon Hughes / Bedrock Studios 22tc; Judith Miller / Ancient Art 2cra, 11tl; Colin Keates / Courtesy of the Natural History Museum, London 3tl, 16cl, 25tr (Sandstone), 27tl, 33bl, 70tl; Dave King / Courtesy of the National Motor Museum, Beaulieu 14tr; Tim Draper / Dave King / Courtesy of The Science Museum, London 10cl, 11tr; Judith Miller / Cooper Owen 9fcl; Judith Miller / Luna 44c; Judith Miller / Toy Road Antiques 23cr; Judith Miller / Wallis &

Wallis 44tl; NASA 50bl; James Stevenson & Tina Chambers / National Maritime Museum, London 4tc, 21cl; Clive Streeter / Courtesy of The Science Museum, London 4cl, 10–11c, 56tr; Linda Whitwam / Courtesy of the Yufuin Folk Art Museum, Japan 60cl; Photograph Courtesy of EFDA-JET: 63cr; Empics Ltd: EPA 45tl; Getty Images: AFP 61crb; Alexander Drozdov / AFP 20cl; Jerry Grayson / Helifilms Australia PTY Ltd. 68br; Paul S. Howell / Liaison 31tl; Hulton Archive 27crb, 48tl; Image Bank / Cousteau Society 33br; Alex Livesey 47tc; Lonely Planet Images / Jim Wark 41tl; Jamie McDonald 47tr; Carl Mydans / Time Life Pictures 48cla; National Geographic / Justin Guariglia 32cl; National Geographic / Sarah Leen 16tl; Mustafa Ozer / AFP 34br; Photographer's Choice / David Seed Photography 57tr; Photographer's Choice / Joe McBride 7tl; Photographer's Choice / Rich LaSalle 71tl; Stone / David Frazier 56–57c; Stone / David Hiser 23cl; Stone / Keith Wood 37tc; Stone / Tom Bean 50crb; Stone + / Tim Macpherson 6tr; Sergei Supinsky / AFP 49c; Texas Energy Museum / Newsmakers 13tr; Three Lions 13tl; Yoshikazu Tsuno / AFP 55cl; Greg Wood / AFP 45tr; Landsat 7 satellite image courtesy of NASA Landsat Project Science Office and USGS National Center for Earth Resources Observation Science: 25tl; Library Of Congress, Washington, D.C.: 13c; F.J. Frost, Port Arthur, Texas 30tl; Warren K. Leffler 48bl; Magenn Power Inc. (www.magenn.com): Chris Radisch 57br; Mary Evans Picture Library: 10tr, 20tl, 46tl; Micro-g Lacoste: 29cr; NASA: 59bl; Dryden Flight Research Center Photo Collection 59c; JPL 34bl; Jeff Schmaltz, MODIS Rapid Response Team, GSFC 19tc; Susan R. Trammell (UNC Charlotte) et al., ESAIC, HST, ESA 19bc; National Geographic Image Collection: 42–43b; The Natural History Museum, London: 25bc, 25br; Michael Long 27cla; Oil Museum of Canada, Oil Springs, Ontario:

12bl; Rex Features: Norm Betts 26cl, 26–27b; SIPA Press 61bc; ROSEN Swiss AG: 34c; Science & Society Picture Library: 27c, 45cl; Science Photo Library: Eye of Science 43tc; Ken M. Johns 25c; Laguna Design 16–17c; Lawrence Livermore Laboratory 63ca; Tony McConnell 53cl; Carlos Munoz-Yague / Eurelios 51br; Alfred Pasieka 53cr; Paul Rapson 6tl, 17br, 39tl; Chris Sattlberger 28cl; Still Pictures: Joerg Boethling 54bl; Mark Edwards 12–13bc; Russell Gordon 30cr; Walter H. Hodge 24–25b; Knut Mueller 66tr; Darlyne A. Murawski 18b; S.Compoint / UNEP 31b; TopFoto.co.uk: HIP / The British Library 9br; Dr Richard Tyson, School of Geoscience and Civil Engineering, Newcastle University: 19clb; © TOTAL UK Limited 2005: 64cr; Vattenfall Group: 56cr; Auke Visser, Holland: 36cb; Wikipedia, The Free Encyclopedia: 2cl, 44tr; Woodside Energy Ltd. (www.woodside.com.au): 5tr, 28cr, 28bl, 29b.

Wallchart
Alamy Images: Bryan & Cherry Alexander Photography (Trans Alaska Pipeline). The Art Archive: (Chinese Oil). Courtesy of BMW: (Hydrogen Car). Corbis: Martin Harvey / Gallo Images (Oil Damaged Bird); Roger Ressmeyer (Oil Refinery). DK Images: Courtesy of The Natural History Museum, London (Sandstone). Getty Images: Photographer's Choice / David Seed Photography (Wind Farm). Science Photo Library: Laguna Design (Hydrocarbon Model). Still Pictures: Russell Gordon (Oil Rig Drill). Woodside Energy Ltd. (www.woodside.com.au): (Survey Truck).

All other images © Dorling Kindersley
For further information see: www.dkimages.com